The U.S. Senate and Strategic Arms Policy, 1969-1977

Westview Replica Editions

This book is a Westview Replica Edition. The concept of Replica Editions is a response to the crisis in academic and informational publishing. Library budgets for books have been severely curtailed; economic pressures on the university presses and the few private publishing companies primarily interested in scholarly manuscripts have severely limited the capacity of the industry to properly serve the academic and research communities. Many manuscripts dealing with important subjects, often representing the highest level of scholarship, are today not economically viable publishing projects. Or, if they are accepted for publication, they are often subject to lead times ranging from one to three years. Scholars are understandably frustrated when they realize that their first-class research cannot be published within a reasonable time frame, if at all.

Westview Replica Editions seem to us one feasible and practical solution to the crisis. The concept is simple. We accept a manuscript in camera-ready form and move it immediately into the production process. The responsibility for textual and copy editing lies with the author or sponsoring organization. If necessary we will advise the author on proper preparation of footnotes and bibliography. The manuscript is acceptable as typed for a thesis or dissertation or prepared in any other clearly organized and readable way, though we prefer it typed according to our specifications. The end result is a book produced by lithography and bound in hard covers. Edition sizes range from 200 to 600 copies. We will include among Westview Replica Editions only works of outstanding scholarly quality or of great informational value and we will exercise our usual editorial standards and quality control.

The U.S. Senate and Strategic Arms Policy

Alan Platt

The role of Congress in shaping U.S. foreign policy has grown significantly in recent years, particularly since the Vietnam involvement and the 1969 ABM debate. This book analyzes congressional participation in one important policy area--strategic arms policy--from 1969 to 1977. The author, who has worked on issues related to SALT in both the legislative and executive branches, discusses in detail the Senate's involvement in the three major strategic arms policy issues that the U.S. government has faced in recent years: SALT I, SALT II, and selective counterforce targeting. In the epilog he compares the Senate's role in SALT during the first year of the Carter Administration with its role during the Nixon-Ford-Kissinger era.

Alan Platt is special assistant for congressional relations, U.S. Arms Control and Disarmament Agency. Previously lecturer in American foreign policy at Stanford University and legislative assistant for foreign affairs to Senator Edmund Muskie, he received his Ph.D. from Columbia University.

The U.S. Senate and Strategic Arms Policy, 1969-1977

Alan Platt

Westview Press / Boulder, Colorado

ST. PHILIPS COLLEGE LIBRARY

A Westview Replica Edition

All rights reserved. No part of this publication may be
reproduced or transmitted in any form or by any means,
electronic or mechanical, including photocopy, recording,
or any information storage and retrieval system, without
permission in writing from the publisher.

Copyright © 1978 by Westview Press, Inc.

Published in 1978 in the United States of America by
   Westview Press, Inc.
   5500 Central Avenue
   Boulder, Colorado   80301
   Frederick A. Praeger, Publisher

Library of Congress Catalog Card Number: 78-7151
ISBN: 0-89125-179-0

TO MY PARENTS

Contents

	List of abbreviations	xi
	Preface	xiii
1	INTRODUCTION	1
2	SALT I, 1969-1972	9
3	SALT II, 1972-1976	37
4	SELECTIVE COUNTERFORCE TARGETING, 1974-1976	71
5	CONCLUSION	97
6	EPILOGUE, 1977	110
	Selected bibliography	119
	Index	125

Abbreviations

ABM	Anti-ballistic missile
ACDA	Arms Control and Disarmament Agency
ALCM	Air-launched cruise missile
FBS	Foreward-based systems
ICBM	Inter-continental ballistic missile
IRBM	Intermediate-range ballistic missile
LTBT	Limited Test Ban Treaty
MBFR	Mutual Balanced Force Reductions (for Central Europe)
MIRV	Multiple independently targetable re-entry vehicle
MLBM	Modern large ballistic missile
MRBM	Medium-range ballistic missile
NATO	North Atlantic Treaty Organization
NPT	Non-Proliferation Treaty
OTA	Office of Technology Assessment
PNE	Peaceful Nuclear Explosion
SALT	Strategic Arms Limitation Talks
SLBM	Submarine-launched ballistic missile
SSBM	Nuclear-powered ballistic missile submarine
TTBT	Threshold Test Ban Treaty

Preface

In the last several years, the United States Senate has played an increasingly active and influential role in the making of American foreign policy. One need only think of the 1973 War Powers Act, legislation initiated in the Senate and passed over a presidential veto, or Congress' ending of U.S. involvement in Indochina and Angola to substantiate this. In the period since the historic ABM debate of 1969, what has been the Senate's role in the area of strategic arms policy-making? This book is intended to shed some light on this question.

The inspiration for this work came during the 1973-74 years while I was Legislative Assistant for Foreign Affairs to Senator Edmund S. Muskie. At the time, Muskie was Chairman of the Foreign Relations Subcommittee on Arms Control. It struck me that there was a real gap between what was being written at universities and think-tanks about the increasingly active congressional role in all aspects of foreign policy, including SALT, and the day-to-day reality of marginal congressional involvement in the strategic arms policy process. In early 1975, I left Senator Muskie's staff to become a Research Associate of Stanford University's Arms Control and Disarmament Program, and in 1975-76 while at Stanford, I completed the bulk of this manuscript. The epilogue, which deals with the Senate's involvement in SALT in 1977, was written while I was Special Assistant for Congressional Relations at the U.S. Arms Control and Disarmament Agency.

This book is an effort to describe and analyze in concrete terms what role the Senate has or has not played in the strategic arms policy process during the 1969-1977 years. It does not pretend to be a comprehensive, exhaustive treatment of the subject. Indeed, it is hoped that this work will stimulate further research on executive-legislative relations in this critical policy area. The book draws heavily on my experience in both the legislative and executive branches, with all the limitations and advantages stemming from an author's direct personal involvement in the subject matter under discussion.

Many people must be thanked for making this work possible. I owe a special debt of gratitude to John Wilson Lewis, Professor of Political Science at Stanford and Director of its Arms Control and Disarmament Program. Early on, John accorded high priority to this project, and amidst an extremely busy schedule, John has given his unstinting support and wise counsel. I also owe thanks to Senator Edmund S. Muskie, my former boss, and Paul C. Warnke, my present boss, for greatly enhancing my understanding of SALT and Congress' role in the SALT process. Special thanks are also due to: Edmund Beard, Dan Caldwell, I.M. Destler, Thomas Dine, Alton Frye, Alexander George, Thomas Halsted, Robert Keohane, Michael Mandelbaum, John Newhouse, Cathie Smith, Gary Wasserman, and Lawrence Weiler, all of whom have read and commented on part or all of the manuscript. A debt of gratitude is also owed to the many people whom I have interviewed for this book. Some of these have agreed to be identified; many, particularly those still working in the government, preferred to remain anonymous. The latter group comprise the "confidential interviews" cited in the footnotes. Finally, I wish to thank Michael Glennon and Lynne Rienner for their editorial assistance, the Ford Foundation for its generous support, and Gerry Bowman for help in preparing the manuscript.

All responsibility for what follows, of course, rests solely with the author, whose views do not necessarily represent those of any agency or institution.

                                                   Alan Platt
                                                   Washington, D.C.
                                                   April 1978

1. Introduction

On August 6, 1969, the United States Senate approved by one vote an administration request to deploy an anti-ballistic missile system. The vote took place after the most searching congressional examination of any military weapons program in the postwar period. Prior to the vote, hearings on the ABM were held by several different committees. Numerous executive branch officials and outside experts testified to and were questioned intensively about the pros and cons of the system. Alternatives to the administration policy were proposed and debated. In all, Congress, although it ultimately approved the administration's request, exhaustively scrutinized the executive's proposed policy for deploying an anti-ballistic missile system.

Following the occasionally heated ABM debate, which lasted for more than five weeks, many senators publicly expressed the view that Congress was entering a new era in regard to legislative involvement in the making of U.S. strategic arms policy.* Murray Marder, veteran diplomatic correspondent of The Washington Post, wrote about the first session of the 91st Congress in the following dramatic way:

> Groundwork for a non-violent rebellion inside the American Establishment was begun during the session of Congress that ended Tuesday. Young militants would hoot at the sedate in-house struggle. But historians do not. They will watch with scholarly fascination to see if the decade of the 70's produces only a sham revolt or a reapportionment of power between the executive and the legislative branches on matters of war and peace....
> The challengers of unquestioned executive branch primacy went on to question intended actions they never dreamed

---

*The term "U.S. strategic arms policy" is used hereafter to refer to that part of American foreign policy which is concerned with our nuclear arsenal.

1

of seriously disputing in years past. They contested and lost by only one vote, the decision to develop an anti-ballistic missile system....[1]

Tom Halsted, then chief anti-ABM lobbyist for the Council for a Livable World, summarized the new situation more succinctly: "The ABM debates have brought about some permanent changes. The public has become involved to an important degree in national security decisionmaking. The days of congressional rubber-stamping may be over."[2]

Underlying these remarks was the feeling, held widely both inside and outside Congress, that from the dawn of the nuclear age in 1945 until the 1969 ABM debate, the legislative branch had largely relinquished oversight responsibility for national security issues to the executive branch, most particularly with regard to arms control matters.[3] Between 1945 and 1969, few members of Congress had been actively involved in the formulation of arms control policy; Congress had generally been content with pro forma evaluation of the executive's annual defense requests, save for an occasional increase in appropriations for a particular weapons system and a still more occasional marginal cut in the Pentagon's annual budget in the name of fiscal prudence. To be sure, there were some exceptions to this pattern of congressional rubber-stamping. But Congress' role in the passage of the McMahon Act of 1954, its interest in the 1956-58 manned bomber versus missile controversy, and its active support of the 1963 Limited Test Ban and the 1968 Non-Proliferation Treaty stand out precisely as exceptions that prove the rule.

The nature and duration of the 1969 ABM debate led many Members of Congress to believe that henceforth the Senate and House would not be the rubber stamp for executive-initiated strategic arms policies that they had consistently been throughout the postwar years. Now, perhaps, the situation was different. No longer, some felt, would executive branch officials be able to testify on Capitol Hill only behind closed doors to field only supportive questions. No longer would Members of Congress and their staffs feel they lacked the necessary background and expertise to understand and discuss U.S. strategic doctrines and policies, and passively accept that status. No longer would the executive branch be the sole source of technical information on complex strategic matters. And, most important, no longer could the executive branch be certain that its ideas on strategic arms policy would receive unquestioned support. John Sherman Cooper, a senior member of the Senate Foreign Relations Committee, expressed the feelings of many of his colleagues at the time of the ABM debate when he philosophically reflected in a speech on the Senate floor that:

The responsibility for national security rests with the

Congress as well as the executive branch of government.
We respect the President's grave responsibilities, but
the Constitution calls for a joint judgment. It is a
trust given the Congress by the people.[4]

Since the ABM debate of 1969, how has Congress fulfilled
this trust? Was the ABM debate and vote a watershed or an
aberrant instance of meaningful congressional involvement in
U.S. strategic arms policy-making.?

The answers to these questions depend, in large part, on
how one defines "meaningful congressional involvement."
Since 1969, many changes and innovations have, in fact,
occurred in the Congress and taken together, they suggest a
new pattern of congressional interest and involvement in the
making of U.S. strategic arms policy. Among other things, the
1969-77 period saw:

(1) an increase in the amount of time Members of Congress
spent at hearings and working on legislation concerning strategic arms issues;
(2) an increase in the number of witnesses from outside
the executive branch called to testify before Congress on such issues;
(3) an increase in the number of witnesses presenting
views different from those of the executive branch;
(4) an increase in the quality and quantity of congressional staff members dealing with foreign policy
issues in general and strategic arms issues in partiular;
(5) an increase in congressional committees' use of technically competent, outside consultants who were once
employees of the executive branch and inclined to
subject the administration's policy preferences to
independent examination;
(6) an increase in the amount of information pertaining
to strategic issues diffused throughout Congress as
a result of vastly expanded committee reports;
(7) an increase in the number of amendments offered to
the annual Military Procurement Authorizations and
Appropriations Bills;
(8) a decrease in the deference paid to the norm of specialization concerning strategic arms issues, and a
concomitant increase in the involvement of more individual senators and representatives and more committees other than the Armed Services Committees (e.g.,
Senate Foreign Relations and House International Relations Committees, Senate and House Budget Committees) in national security issues.[5]

In addition, in the 1969-77 period, Congress attempted
to upgrade the national security capabilities of two existent
organizations--the General Accounting Office and the Congres-

sional Research Service of the Library of Congress. During these years, Congress also set up two new organizations capable of providing in-depth analyses of various weapons systems--the Office of Technology Assessments (OTA) and the Congressional Budget Office (CBO).

Besides these congressionally inspired efforts, after the ABM debate there was a concerted movement outside the government to heighten congressional knowledge about and interest in national security issues. Specifically, several private organizations--the Federation of American Scientists, Members of Congress for Peace Through Law, Arms Control Association, Council for a Livable World, and the Center for Defense Information--were either energized or created to supply Members of Congress with, *inter alia*, detailed information about U.S. strategic arms policies.

These developments all suggest that since 1969 there has been a change in the magnitude of congressional interest and involvement in the strategic arms policy-making process. However, in order to pass judgment on the question of whether recent congressional involvement has been "meaningful," it seems necessary to examine an additional, perhaps more fundamental, dimension of the issue--the quality (i.e., depth, continuity) of this legislative involvement. Specifically, it seems necessary to go beyond the measurement of quantitative indicators demonstrating increased congressional involvement to consideration of such questions as:

-Did Congress keep itself informed about and press administration officials to explain the executive branch's proposed policies?

-Did Congress question and debate the executive branch's goals and the bases underlying these goals?

-Did Congress, in considering the executive branch's proposed initiatives, build public understanding of the policy issues involved?

-Did Congress develop and consider alternatives to administration policies?

-Did Congress participate in setting the general direction of policy, leaving the day-to-day management of policy to the executive?

-Did Congress hold executive branch officials accountable for their stewardship?

In this study, the Senate's role is discussed in regard to the three major strategic arms policy issues that the U.S. government dealt with since 1969: SALT I, SALT II, and selective counterforce targeting. The first two cases focus on the U.S. negotiating posture in arms talks with the Soviet Union, while the third deals with the establishment of new doctrinal policy and appropriations to implement that policy. In analyzing each of these three cases, there is an attempt to shed light on the Senate's role in terms of the above-noted, six interrelated criteria for "meaningful congressional involvement." In all of the cases, the primary purpose of the discussion is not to explore the substantive policy issues involved, but rather, to analyze the nature of the legislative branch's involvement in the process by which U.S. policy was made in the particular cases under discussion.

Chapters 2 and 3 deal with the role of the Senate in SALT I and SALT II respectively. Chapter 4 focuses on the Senate's role in the promulgation and implementation of a U.S. policy of selective counterforce targeting, a policy ardently espoused by former Defense Secretary James Schlesinger during 1974-75. Specifically, this policy, which calls for greater selectivity and flexibility in the nation's targeting doctrine, led the executive branch to request monies from the Congress in Fiscal Years 1975, 1976, and 1977 to increase the accuracy and yield of our warheads.

The major finding of the study is that on close examination, in the cases of SALT I and SALT II, in the 1969-76 years, the executive branch by and large shaped U.S. policy while the Congress consistently acquiesced in executive dominance. Specifically, in both of these cases, the executive branch formulated a policy course for the country, selectively consulted with and released information to the Congress, and basically expected and received legislative support. The Congress, in its turn, largely abdicated its oversight responsibility and made little meaningful effort to analyze, debate, or explore alternatives to the policies proposed by the executive branch. Typically, the large majority of senators and representatives opted not even to inform themselves about the precise nature of the issues which the country was facing, let alone challenge executive branch policy. In short, in both of these cases, Congress' performance was a far cry from Senator Cooper's proposed "joint judgment." By contrast, the process by which U.S. selective counterforce targeting policy was made and carried out was characterized by relatively more meaningful legislative involvement. In this case, the policy process involved the executive branch asking Congress for appropriations to implement policy and necessarily providing the legislative branch with a significant amount of information to support the requested appropriations.

Chapter 5 is an effort to explain the varying degrees of Senate involvement in these three cases during the 1969-76 years and analyzes Senate involvement in strategic arms policy matters in terms of the attitude, organization, and operation of both the legislative and executive branches.

The epilogue focuses on Senate involvement in the SALT II policy process in 1977, contrasting the Senate's role in SALT during the first year of the Carter Administration with the Nixon-Ford-Kissinger era.

One caveat should be noted in regard to all of these discussions: the emphasis is on the actions of the Senate, not of the entire Congress. Where appropriate, the interests and involvement of the House of Representatives and its relevant committees and subcommittees are discussed as well as those of the Senate. By and large, congressional involvement in strategic arms policy-making in the 1969-77 years was Senate involvement and mainly individual senators' involvement at that. Accordingly, the discussions and analyses concentrate on the Senate as a whole, the two most responsible Senate committees (e.g., Foreign Relations, Armed Services), and the activities of individual senators.

In the preface to A Responsible Congress,[6] Alton Frye recounts the comment of a senator to an executive branch witness at a recent congressional hearing: "You are making progress more difficult by refusing to recognize its achievement." Throughout his book, Frye takes the view that there has been altogether too much criticism of Congress and now those who believe in an expanded role for Congress in the foreign affairs field should recognize the legislative branch's virtues and acclaim its new vitality in this realm.

The implicit bias of this study is the same as Frye's: Congress has a constitutionally legitimate and politically important role to play in the formulation of U.S. strategic arms policy. However, the conclusions we draw from recent executive-legislative relations in this area differ considerably. For while Frye and others[7] cite a variety of quantitative indicators and personal anecdotes to demonstrate and applaud increased legislative involvement in strategic arms policy-making, Senate involvement in this policy area in the 1969-76 years was, in fact, superficial, rather than substantive; marginal, rather than central; more concerned with form than content. The result was that the executive branch during the 1969-76 period largely dominated the decision-making process in this policy area.

To be sure, there are definite limits to the role that Congress can and ought to play in the formulation and execution of the U.S. strategic arms policy. Obviously, on some national security issues, there are times when it is important for the United States to speak with one voice in an unequivocal manner. On other national security issues, there are times when the government must act with dispatch. And on most national security issues, it is necessary for the executive to initiate policies and for the government to be able to react flexibly to changing world conditions. Additionally, on virtually all foreign policy matters, the executive branch is better suited than the Congress to pursue day-by-day initiatives, particularly as they concern negotiations with other nations.

To make these points, though, is not to deny Congress an important role in the making of U.S. strategic arms policy. The fact is that Congress is necessarily involved in the process by which all of our foreign policy is made through the appropriations process. The Founding Fathers, upset with arbitrary rule and high taxation, gave the power of the purse to the legislative branch. Representatives, they felt, would be more responsive to public needs than a potentially arbitrary executive. Specifically, Article I of the Constitution unequivocally states that "no money shall be drawn from the Treasury, but on Consequence of Appropriations made by Law; and a regular Statement and Account of the Receipts and Expenditures of all public Money shall be published from time to time."

Regarding strategic arms policies, each year during the postwar period Congress has appropriated millions--and now billions--of dollars for various weapons systems designed to support a given set of strategic policies. Most of the time these systems have been explicitly requested and justified by the executive branch as essential to the maintenance of the national defense. During both SALT I and SALT II, certain additional monies for weapons systems have been sought and justified as being necessary bargaining chips, i.e., systems to be negotiated away in prospective international talks to limit strategic arms. In all cases, Congress, in annually appropriating monies for the national defense, has had to make many trade-offs and judgments regarding the country's priorities. And it is in making these judgments and trade-offs that Congress' constitutional responsibilities and real strength lie. For if the legislative branch has a legitimate role to play in the formulation of national policy, it is especially in those areas where questions of priorities are to be determined, where decisions have to be made about how the nation's monies are to be spent.

Surprisingly, Congress frequently has only dimly perceived the budgetary trade-offs and decisions on priorities inherently contained within each year's appropriation for strategic programs. But these trade-offs and decisions surely have been there. Indeed, the sums of money have been so great and the issues associated with making the necessary choices in this policy so important--both in terms of dollars and in terms of their potential for war and peace--that it seems remarkable Congress has not involved itself more consciously in the strategic arms policy-making process.

In recent years there has been an enormous amount of criticism of Congress, some of it justified and some not. To those interested in seeing the legislative branch play a meaningful role in the strategic arms area in particular and the foreign affairs field in general, further critical analysis should be welcome. Only by describing, analyzing, and understanding what Congress has and has not done in recent years can one hope to prescribe what might be done in the future to maintain a constitutional balance between the two branches in regard to the nation's strategic arms policies.

NOTES

1. The Washington Post, December 27, 1969, p. A-2.
2. Thomas Halsted, "Lobbying Against the ABM, 1967-70," Bulletin of the Atomic Scientists 27 (April 1971): 28.
3. For the purposes of this study, the term "arms control" refers to "limitations on the numbers or types of armaments or armed forces, on their deployment or disposition, or on the use of particular types of armaments." This definition is borrowed from the Stanford University Arms Control Group's International Arms Control: Issues and Agreements, John H. Barton and Lawrence Weiler (eds.) (Stanford, California: Stanford University Press, 1976), p. 3.
4. Congressional Record, August 6, 1969, p. S22488.
5. For additional indicators of increased congressional involvement in national security policy in recent years, see Anne Cahn, "Congress, Military Affairs and Information," Sage Publication #04-017 (Beverly Hills, 1974), pp. 46-48.
6. Alton Frye, A Responsible Congress (New York: McGraw Hill, 1975).
7. See Edward Laurance, "The Changing Role of Congress in Defense Policy-Making," Journal of Conflict Resolution (June 1976): 213-53. See also, Anne Cahn, "Congress, Military Affairs and Information," and James Clotfelter, The Military in American Politics (Chapel Hill: University of North Carolina Press, 1973), pp. 148-81.

2. SALT I, 1969-1972

The first session of SALT I began on November 17, 1969 in Helsinki. The talks were to last two and one-half years and alternate between Helsinki and Vienna. In all, there were seven sessions to SALT I.

On November 12, the week before the talks began, Senator Albert Gore, chairman of the Foreign Relations Subcommittee on Arms Control, publicly announced that he would have to cancel a closed-door subcommittee briefing on SALT. Gore explained that Gerard Smith, the Director of the Arms Control and Disarmament Agency (ACDA) and chief U.S. SALT negotiator, had telephoned earlier that day to say that he was not "free" to discuss with Members of Congress any of the specifics of U.S. SALT policy.[1] Nettled by his conversation with Smith, Gore fervently expressed the hope that thereafter Congress would play an active role in SALT in particular and foreign policy in general and that the Nixon Administration would help in this endeavor. Following Gore's statement, it was reported that prior to cancelling the briefing, Smith had talked to Presidential Assistant for National Security Affairs Henry Kissinger and that the White House had "vetoed" the idea of Smith's testifying.[2]

The following day, after a breakfast meeting with President Nixon, Senate Majority Leader Mike Mansfield announced that there had been a "misunderstanding" which he thought was now "cleared up."[3] But, on the same day, President Nixon, while acknowledging the importance of keeping the Senate fully informed on SALT matters, publicly declared that it was "vital that we recognize that the position of our negotiators not be weakened or compromised by discussions that might take place here [in Congress]."[4]

The unavailability of a key executive branch official to brief Congress on the specifics of SALT;[5] the subsequent, ineffectual grumbling of a few members of the Senate Foreign Relations Committee (e.g., Gore, Cooper, Case) about the cancelled Smith hearing and about Congress being inadequately informed about national security matters; the lip service the

Nixon Administration paid to the idea of keeping Congress fully informed about SALT--this series of events that took place before the first session of the SALT negotiations had even been convened was in many ways characteristic of executive-legislative relations during the entire SALT I negotiations. The executive branch publicly supported the idea that Congress be fully informed about and closely involved in the SALT process, while briefing Congress in a generally pro forma way and discussing some of the details of SALT with selected senators and a few representatives only on those rare occasions when the Nixon Administration felt that it would be advantageous to do so. The legislative branch, in its turn, periodically complained about inadequate information, consultation and involvement regarding SALT but did very little, in practice, to oversee or affect the executive's dominant role in the SALT policy-making process.

The lack of significant congressional knowledge about or involvement in the process by which the United States government formulated policy on SALT matters was apparent long before November 1969. During the first ten months of 1969, the newly installed Nixon Administration hammered out--without informing Congress--various options for the U.S. SALT negotiating team and, at the same time, established the governmental machinery by which U.S. SALT policy was to be made. On January 21, the day after Nixon's inauguration, Presidential Assistant Kissinger issued a National Security Study Memorandum (NSSM), assigning the executive branch bureaucracy the task of looking at the criteria against which American military needs were to be measured. Titled "Military Posture," NSSM #3 was to look at U.S. forces vis à vis those of the Soviet Union. Some two months later, despite objections from the Joint Chiefs of Staff, Kissinger issued another National Security Study Memorandum, NSSM #28, which directed the bureaucracy to come up with various options for future strategic arms limitations talks. As John Newhouse has summarily noted, NSSM #28 would show what limitations the United States could accept or propose that did not intrude upon the needs of the military. In theory, "NSSM 3 was the root, NSSM 28 the stem."[6]

The machinery for making U.S. policy on SALT was put into place more slowly because this involved the sensitive matter of transferring control over key SALT decisions from the executive branch bureaucracy to the White House. It was not until mid-summer of 1969 that the bureaucracy had, in fact, been circumvented and the formal mechanisms for SALT policy-making were centralized in the White House.

Specifically, in July 1969, at Kissinger's suggestion the Nixon Administration established a SALT Verification Panel Working Group charged with reviewing all the strategic implications of SALT. Membership of the Verification Panel included: Presidential Assistant Kissinger, who acted as chairman; ACDA Director and chief SALT negotiator Smith; Under Secretary of State Elliot Richardson; Deputy Secretary of Defense David Packard; Chairman of the Joint Chiefs of Staff Earle Wheeler; CIA Director Richard Helms; and Attorney General John Mitchell. Lawrence Lynn, senior White House staff member on SALT, was chosen to chair the Working Group. As Kissinger subsequently noted:

> The Verification Panel analyzed each of the weapons systems which could conceivably be involved in an agreement. It compared the effect of different limitations on our program and on the Soviet programs, and weighed the resulting balance. It analyzed the possibilities of verification and the precise risk of evasion, seeking to determine at which point evasion could be detected and what measures would be available for a response.[7]

What Kissinger did not say publicly was that the Verification Panel and the associated decision-making machinery allowed the president's Assistant for National Security Affairs to define the shape of the SALT issues being considered by the government; to specify what alternatives existed; and, ultimately, to present choices to the President for his "decision."[8] Thus, on the substance of key SALT issues, the terms of the discussion were narrowly established and controlled by Henry Kissinger. William Van Cleave, a former member of the negotiating team for SALT I, summarized the decision-making process in the following way:

> In the preparation for and management of SALT, the White House retained the principal role. Dr. Kissinger and his staff decided the work to be done, the issues to be addressed, the agendas of inter-agency meetings and usually the wording of directives, whether ad hoc or in the forms of NSDM's--Presidential decision memoranda.[9]

The Verification Panel machinery produced exhaustive studies on both the issues involved at SALT and possible U.S. positions at the negotiations. Initially, nine options were recommended for the negotiating team. The options were, in fact, seen as "building blocks," rather than complete formal alternative policy positions. The idea was that part of each option (e.g., MIRV limitations, suspension of ABM deployment, ban on mobile land-based missiles, et al.) could be shuffled into and out of various negotiating stances depending upon the response of the Soviet Union. The executive branch justified this approach to SALT on the grounds that it left our negotiators with a great deal of flexibility to mix numbers and deployments of various weapons systems and meant that various alternatives could be discussed without a renegotiation in Washington of the entire U.S. position.[10]

The first session of SALT I lasted a little more than a month; the American negotiating team returned to Washington three days before Christmas. The initial round of talks ended with a short communiqué which declared that "an understanding was reached on the general range of questions which will be the subject of further U.S.-Soviet exchanges."[11] The talks were set to resume in Vienna on April 16, 1970, some four months hence.

With the initial exploratory session out of the way at which no specific proposals were presented by either side, Kissinger sent a memo on December 30, 1969 to the Verification Panel. In the memo, Kissinger posed several key questions:

> What levels of ABM's are required for protection against accidental and third country attacks, for protection of the U.S. bomber force, for defense of Minutemen and for the defense of the National Command Authority [the capital]?
>
> What are the verification problems and strategic implications of possible upgrading of Soviet air defense missiles to give them ABM capabilities and of their ABM systems to give them more extensive capabilities?
>
> What would be the consequences for the United States and allied security of an agreement which does not place limits on intermediate range missiles?
>
> What are the strategic and verification implications of restricting ballistic missile submarine patrols and the overseas flights of strategic aircraft?[12]

During the first two months of 1970, the SALT bureaucracy worked up answers to these and related questions. When the staff work was completed, President Nixon and Kissinger invited eight senators and seven representatives to the White House on March 16, 1970 for a secret briefing. According to one observer this was "the most detailed briefing on SALT the congressional leadership was to receive until the President returned from Moscow more than two years later with the agreements themselves."[13] At the briefing, which was presented by the president, Kissinger, Rogers, Laird, Helms, and General Wheeler, four options for our SALT negotiating team were described. Following some questions, the President announced that the so-called "high options" C and D had been selected. Option C--a MIRV ban policed by on-site inspectors and a limit of one ABM deployment around the national capital (NCA)-- was to be offered first. If the Russians rejected this proposal, Option D was then to be put forward--a phasing down of land-based ICBMs, no limitation on MIRVs, and a limit of one

ABM deployment around the national capital. If the ABM part of either Option C or D was not accepted by the Soviets, the negotiators were instructed to propose a ban on all ABM deployments.

The response of the congressional audience was that of an uninformed, disinterested audience. The senators and representatives were told about various policy options and then told which options had been chosen and why. Prior to the briefing, few of the congressional participants knew much about SALT beyond what had appeared in the media in the form of speculation. More importantly, even fewer were disposed to press the executive branch officials about the administration's specific goals in SALT or the assumptions behind those objectives. Hence, such questions as why the national capital option was to be offered prior to offering a total ban of ABMs or whether there was any possibility that the Soviets would respond positively to on-site inspectors were not even raised. Rather, when the president announced that Options C and D had been selected, the response was "positive, congratulatory, and, in a few cases, even enthusiastic."[14]

Unfortunately, but perhaps predictably, the Soviet response was not uniformly enthusiastic. On the one hand, the NCA/ABM proposal in Option C was accepted by the Soviets within one week of its presentation. On the other hand, the U.S. MIRV proposal was rejected soon after it was introduced. The Soviets felt that it would freeze them into a technologically inferior position as well as impose on-site inspectors, a condition they found unacceptable.[15] In response, the Soviets proposed a ban on MIRV production and deployment. But this proposal, which did not include a ban on MIRV testing, was unacceptable to the United States.

Following the Soviet delegation's rejection of Option C, Option D was offered by the American delegation. It was emphatically rejected by the Soviets. This proposal, they felt (quite rightly), would diminish the strongest part of the Soviet arsenal--land-based ICBMs--and force them to move out to sea where the United States enjoyed a significant advantage. At the same time, it would allow the United States to continue its planned MIRVing of American missile forces but would not limit the U.S. forward-based systems in Europe. The Soviets, therefore, accepted the idea of limiting ABM deployments to one site around the national capital, and rejected both of our offensive weapons proposals. The talks went no further, and Smith and his fellow negotiators returned to Washington from Vienna in mid-June 1970.

While the second round of SALT was in progress in Vienna, an effort had been made in the Senate to influence the U.S. negotiating position in the talks, particularly as it concerned MIRVs. The Senate's actions, however, proved to be ineffectual--in part because of the character of the Senate's response and in part because the Congress did not really know the nature of the Administration's MIRV proposal.[16]

Two weeks before the American delegation left for Vienna, March 10, 1970, Air Force Secretary Robert Seamans, in testimony before the Senate Armed Services Committee, announced that the administration would begin deploying MIRVs in June of that year.[17] The year before, on June 17, 1969, Senator Edward Brooke had introduced Senate Resolution 211, which called on the president to propose a joint American-Soviet moratorium on MIRV flight testing. The resolution, which had 39 co-sponsors, was referred to the Foreign Relations Committee but languished there. Several of the committee members felt that reporting out the resolution would interfere with the executive's negotiating efforts at SALT. And most members felt, as Senator Gore did, that the administration should continue research and development on MIRVs and that the executive branch "would await some reasonable determination of the possibilities of agreement [at SALT] before actual deployment of MIRV."[18]

Following the Seamans announcement, which was subsequently described by the administration as having "slipped through" the Pentagon, the Foreign Relations Subcommittee on Arms Control convened in mid-March 1970 a series of hearings to examine MIRVs and ABMs and their relation to SALT and the nuclear arms race. The first two witnesses called were Senator Brooke and Marshall Shulman, a well-known Columbia University expert on Soviet-American relations. These two men, as well as a host of succeeding witnesses, urged quick adoption of Senate Resolution 211--both to encourage "an immediate effort to arrange a MIRV moratorium in the April session of the SALT talks in Vienna and to promote a comprehensive U.S. proposal in those discussions."[19] The committee acted quickly and approved, 10-0, on March 20, 1969 a modified form of Senate Resolution 211. The resolution called on the president to propose to the Soviets an immediate mutual suspension of the further deployment of all offensive and defensive strategic nuclear systems. The resolution, less restrictive in its language concerning MIRVs than Brooke's original legislation, would have allowed the Soviet Union to arrive at a similar MIRV testing level as the United States but would have frozen all activities at that point.

The day after the committee had approved Senate Resolution 211, President Nixon was asked at a press conference about the significance of the legislation. The president responded in categorical terms: "I think the Resolution really is irrelevant to what we are going to do."[20]

Seemingly undaunted by the president's overt disdain for the sense-of-the-Senate legislation, Senate supporters of the legislation pushed hard for action by the entire body. On April 9, 1970, two days after Senate Minority Leader and Nixon loyalist Hugh Scott announced he would be the 51st sponsor of the legislation, the Senate passed Senate Resolution 211 by a vote of 72-6.

Despite the overwhelming margin of the vote, the passage of this legislation had no binding effect and little practical influence on the executive branch. In terms of the talks in Vienna, as one observer has noted, "the Administration showed its contempt for any Senate sentiment by making a facetious proposal at the SALT talks for a MIRV ban, accompanied by mutual verification by inspection, a move Nixon and Kissinger knew the Soviet Union would never accept."[21] William Van Cleave, a member of the SALT negotiating team, has offered a slightly different interpretation of the rationale behind the administration's MIRV proposal. In testimony before the Congress in 1972, Van Cleave suggested that the administration's MIRV proposals at SALT "were not set forth for bargaining, as can be seen by the rapidity with which they were dropped by the United States." Rather, for Van Cleave, these proposals were advanced "to describe preferred end results and to provide a record--for the United States Congress and public-- that at last the United States tried to get MIRV limitations."[22] In any case, as a subsequent Foreign Relations Committee report noted, "the administration rejected this advice by the Senate and continued deployments of nuclear weapons during the process of negotiations."[23]

Despite the executive's seeming indifference toward, if not contempt for, Senate Resolution 211, many senators felt that the Congress had fulfilled its oversight and advisory responsibility on SALT with the passage of this legislation. Indeed, a majority of the Senate seemed to feel that any further congressional efforts to influence the U.S. negotiating position at SALT would tie the hands of our negotiators and seriously impede the possibilities for progress at the Vienna talks. Alton Frye summarized the views of many Members of Congress after the passage of Senate Resolution 211 when he wrote: "The President now enjoyed the broadest reasonable mandate to pursue a negotiated agreement of maximum scope. In realistic political terms the Senate had done about all it could to spur diplomacy."[24]

Following the SALT delegation's return to Washington in mid-June, the Verification Panel undertook an intensive policy review of the U.S. position at SALT. Some ten days later a new option, Option E, surfaced as a result of this review. Closely reflecting Henry Kissinger's views, Option E did away with a proposed MIRV ban, for "Kissinger assumed the Russians would not agree to a moratorium on MIRV's."[25] It also did away with the phased reductions in land-based ICBMs detailed in Option D and instead called for: a mutual limit of 1900 strategic missiles and bombers, with a sublimit of 250 SS-9s and a total ban on land-mobile ICBMs; a prohibition on modifying silos; and a ceiling of 100 ABMs for the defense of either Washington or Moscow, or no ABMs at all.[26]

To gain support for this proposal and, more immediately, to shore up legislative backing for the administration's FY

1971 Safeguard budget request, Kissinger decided that a large-scale briefing of congressional leaders was needed. Accordingly, Kissinger's staff telephoned thirteen senators and thirteen representatives to invite them to a top-level SALT briefing. The meeting was set for July 23, the same day Smith and his colleagues in Vienna were to make an informal presentation of Option E to their Soviet counterparts.

On July 22, Kissinger met with the Senate Republican leadership at the White House. In the conversation, the presidential assistant explained Option E and emphasized the importance of full congressional funding for the administration's annual defense request. The following day, making a rare trip to Capitol Hill, Kissinger met secretly with the invited senators and representatives in a room off the Senate floor of the Capitol to discuss the new SALT proposal and the administration's defense request. Among the attendees were Senators Aiken, Cooper, Fulbright, and Stennis and House leaders McCormack and Albert.

The meeting did not go as well as Kissinger had anticipated. The attendance, which was poor, was made even worse by several rollcall votes. Senator Fulbright, miffed at being "consulted" on the same day that the new proposal was being presented to the Soviets, asked Kissinger rhetorically: "[in terms of consultation] why is your obligation so much heavier to NATO than to the Congress of the United States?"[27] And the following day, Senator Case complained publicly that he could not get the Arms Control and Disarmament Agency to give him a briefing on SALT.[28]

More troubling to the executive branch, the following day there were also accounts of the Capitol Hill meeting in both The New York Times and The Washington Post. Both news articles stressed the fact that Kissinger used the briefing to try to build support for Safeguard on the grounds that the system was a vital bargaining chip in the SALT talks. The Washington Post story, which was the more specific of the two, suggested that Kissinger argued for Safeguard as the way to persuade the Russians to limit their SS-9 program.[29] Infuriated, Kissinger immediately denounced the press accounts of the briefing and Congress' seeming breach of secrecy. Thereafter, Kissinger invoked the principle of executive privilege when asked to testify and did not give a large-scale SALT briefing to members of Congress until after the conclusion of the SALT I accords. Indeed, Kissinger's subsequent dealings with Congress on strategic arms policy matters were principally limited to private discussions with a few individual senators and representatives.

Although the July 23 briefing was something less than a total success, it did help bring some positive results. Three weeks after the briefing, the Senate took up and passed, 52-47, new authorization monies for the Safeguard system. In the course of the floor debate, administration supporters relied heavily on the Kissinger-enunciated bargaining-chip argument. And on the day of the vote, August 12, Gerard Smith was persuaded by Kissinger to send a telegram from Vienna to the Senate, declaring that strong congressional support for continued ABM deployment authorizations would likely expedite the successful conclusion of a SALT I accord. Kissinger's and Smith's bargaining-chip arguments seemed to be decisive, and the August 1970 vote marked the end of major congressional debate over deployment of ABMs.30 Senator Edward Brooke, who previously had been critical of the ABM program, typified congressional sentiment in 1971 when he declared a "personal moratorium" on criticizing the ABM program. In an August speech in Boston, Brooke declared:

> Particularly in view of the delicate diplomacy now underway, I do not believe it would be helpful for the Senate to resurrect last year's controversy over [ABM].... Accordingly, I will not support or participate in extended debate on the ABM.31

Back in Vienna, SALT I was not going as well as the administration had hoped. Specifically, the Soviets, quite aware that the new U.S. proposal did not include limitations on American MIRV programs, were not receptive to the kind of agreement called for in Option E.

Most of the next several months were taken up with each side fencing with the other, scoring debating points and reiterating the basic attitudes of their respective governments. Frustrated by the lack of movement at SALT and aware that a strategic arms accord would enhance his prospects in the imminent 1972 presidential elections, Nixon, through Kissinger, initiated in January 1971 a series of secret or "back-channel" communications with the top Soviet leadership. These communications led directly to the first major breakthrough on SALT some five months later. The highly secret communications, unbeknownst to the U.S. SALT delegation, all of Congress, the American people, and almost all of the executive branch, began on January 9, 1971, when both Nixon and Kissinger met individually with Soviet Ambassador to the United States Anatoly Dobrynin to discuss SALT. In this and subsequent meetings the point was made unequivocally clear to Dobrynin that the United States would insist on a link between offensive and defensive weapons.32 It was reported that in a later meeting, President Nixon gave Dobrynin a personal message for Premier Alexei Kosygin that helped to break the seemingly deadlocked talks.33

In any case, on May 20, 1971, in a noontime television address to the American people, President Nixon announced "a major step in breaking the stalemate on nuclear arms [which has] been deadlocked for over a year." The key part of Nixon's statement read as follows:

17

The Governments of the United States and the Soviet Union, after reviewing the course of their talks on the limitation of strategic armaments, have agreed to concentrate this year on working on an agreement for the limitation of the deployment of antiballistic missile systems.... They have also agreed that, together with concluding an agreement to limit ABM's, they will agree on certain measures with respect to the limitation of offensive strategic weapons.[34]

The American people were, in general, pleased with the president's announcement about progress at SALT. The same was true for most Members of Congress who, like the American people, first learned of the "breakthrough" via television.

There was a small group within the Senate, however, that was concerned about the lack of concrete progress at SALT and the concurrent administration effort to deploy MIRVs. Senator Hubert Humphrey, a long-time advocate of arms control and back in the Senate in 1971 after spending four years as Vice President and two years in private life, spearheaded an effort among his colleagues to limit MIRV deployment. Humphrey, as well as Senators Fulbright, Muskie, and Cooper, feared that continuing MIRV deployment would lead to significant increases in arms spending on both sides and would, ultimately, jeopardize the successful conclusion of a SALT I agreement. Accordingly, in September 1971, Humphrey offered an amendment to the Fiscal Year 1972 Military Procurement Authorization Bill which would have, in essence, frozen MIRVs. His amendment mandated that all funds for MIRV deployment be placed in escrow "until the President and the Congress jointly determine that the Government of the Union of Soviet Socialist Republic's testing and deploying of its own MIRV system and other action necessitate the further testing and deployment of the United States MIRV as a guarantee of the United States' retaliatory capability."[35] Unfortunately for Humphrey and his allies, the Senate leadership brought the amendment up for a vote on a Friday when many potential supporters were absent, and Humphrey's so-called "escrow" amendment was roundly defeated, 39-12.

It should be added that even if the Humphrey amendment had been passed by the Senate and subsequently enacted into law, there is some question about the operational significance of the legislation. The fact is that by the time Humphrey offered the amendment--the summer of 1971--the Strategic Air Command had taken over control of the first ten Minuteman III missiles and the Navy had completed the conversion of the USS James Madison to carry MIRVed-Poseidon missiles. As Ted Greenwood has suggested in his study of U.S. decision-making concerning MIRV, the reaction of congressional critics to MIRV was "too little and too late...the second round of SALT (April-June 1970) was probably the last chance at negotiating a MIRV ban."[36]

During the period from the May 1971 announcement of a "breakthrough at SALT" until President Nixon visited Moscow a year later to sign the SALT I accords, numerous proposals to limit offensive and defensive arms were intensively discussed—within the U.S. executive branch, between the American and Soviet delegations in Vienna and Helsinki—but not in any detail between the U.S. executive branch and Congress. In Washington, the U.S. SALT bureaucracy produced several ABM proposals, at one point even hoping to get an agreement permitting installations at four American ICBM sites and one Soviet site in Moscow—an American "defense"-of-the-deterrent program in exchange for Soviet "defense" of Moscow. As for offensive weapons limitations, there were about as many views in Washington on possible ICBM and SLBM agreements as there were bureaucratic actors within the executive branch, and in the May 1971-May 1972 period several different proposals were explored with the Soviets.[37]

For the most part, Congress did not follow, or even know about, the various proposals under discussion within the executive branch. As in the 1969-71 period, most senators and representatives were inclined to sit back and allow the executive branch to pursue SALT with a free hand, with no "interference" from the legislative branch. Members of the Senate Armed Services and Foreign Relations Committees—those congressional committees most interested in SALT—were content to receive periodic pro forma, reportorial briefings from Gerard Smith, CIA Director Richard Helms, and lesser administration officials dealing with SALT; these usually took place just after the conclusion of a round of talks with the Soviets. Senators with no membership on any of the committees that had jurisdiction over foreign and defense matters were generally limited in their knowledge of SALT to what they read in the newspapers and were reluctant to try to involve themselves in such a sensitive and complex issue. There was also a widespread feeling in Congress, as evidenced by the 1970 ABM and MIRV debates, that if the legislative branch attempted to involve itself closely in the formulation of U.S. SALT policy and tried to explore alternative postures for the American SALT negotiating team, there was a real risk that the successful conclusion of the talks would be jeopardized.[38]

Particularly noteworthy among those Members of Congress who did not share these views were two senators: Republican John Sherman Cooper of Kentucky, a senior member of the Foreign Relations Committee, and Democrat Henry Jackson of Washington, a senior member of the Armed Services Committee. Holding a view quite different from most of his colleagues, Senator Cooper was convinced that it was the constitutional responsibility of the Senate—particularly members of the Foreign Relations Committee—to play an active role in the SALT policy process. In Washington, Cooper frequently met with executive officials--both formally and informally--to discuss strategic issues and, in several instances, to try to help speed the strategic arms negotiations to a successful conclusion. On a few occasions, Cooper even traveled to Helsinki and Vienna to get a first-hand impression of the atmosphere surrounding the talks. However, both in Washington and on these visits, Cooper was limited in what he could do or learn. He had no official connection with the U.S. SALT delegation and at the U.S.-Soviet talks in Europe, he was not even allowed to attend SALT plenary sessions as an observer.

Early in SALT, Cooper, dissatisfied with this arrangement for "consultation," tried to persuade the administration to allow senators to participate directly in SALT, either as observers or as official members of the American delegation. Citing constitutional and pragmatic grounds, Cooper argued that the administration ultimately would have to submit any SALT treaty to the Senate for ratification and felt favorable Senate action on any such agreement would be far more likely if the Congress were brought into the negotiating process at an early date.[39] In these arguments, Cooper and like-minded Members of Congress were rebuffed by the administration. One former National Security Council staff member has since admitted that several administration officials, including Gerard Smith, were sympathetic to the idea of having Cooper and other interested senators participate directly in the SALT talks, particularly during the last six months leading up to the May 1972 summit in Moscow, but that Henry Kissinger strongly opposed congressional participation, and the presidential assistant's views were the administration's on this matter, much to the chagrin of Cooper, Mansfield, and several other senators.[40]

Although differing from Cooper on the substance of many defense issues, Senator Henry Jackson was the only other Member of the Congress who strove to involve himself deeply and directly in the SALT policy-making process. Jackson, a long-time student of national security affairs within the Congress, assumed in December 1969 the chairmanship of a newly-created Armed Services Subcommittee on SALT. Through the chairmanships of this subcommittee and the Government Operations Subcommittee on National Security and International Operations,[41] Jackson attempted to follow closely and influence U.S. policy on SALT matters; he was only partially successful. During the 1969 ABM debate, Jackson was the leading spokesman on the Senate floor for the administration's position. Armed with data supplied by the Defense Department and the CIA, Jackson masterfully used the executive branch's hypothetical projections about the capabilities of the Soviets' SS-9s to argue that four ABM sites were needed to insure the survivability of the U.S. Minuteman force. In 1970, administration officials kept in close touch with the Washington Senator about U.S. strategic policy and he, in turn, successfully led the pro-administration forces within the Senate during the debate on MIRV deployment.

This situation changed in 1971. At that time, with Safeguard funding seemingly secure and the administration considering ABM proposals for less than four sites, key executive officials, led by Henry Kissinger, purposefully attempted to limit Jackson's knowledge of the details of the emerging U.S. policy on SALT, at one point even refusing to discuss what data they had used to estimate future Soviet force levels.[42] This, of course, infuriated Jackson, particularly when it became clear that the administration was leaning toward accepting a 2-American-site to 2-Soviet-site ABM proposal, rather than the 4-American-site to 1-Soviet-site proposal which Jackson had strongly supported. At a congressional hearing in early 1972, Jackson decried the White House's recent reluctance to provide him with detailed information about SALT, sardonically remarking: "When the administration wanted my help on getting the ABM through Congress, it didn't hesitate when I asked about the consequences of the Soviets developing a missile as accurate as our Minuteman."[43] In sum, once the administration was confident funding for the ABM was secure, executive officials, particularly those closest to the negotiations, did not provide the chairman of the Senate Subcommittee on SALT with the kind of information and input on SALT policy issues that he sought and to which he had become accustomed. As a result, during the period immediately leading up to the conclusion of the SALT I accords, Jackson's information about the details of the forthcoming agreement was scanty and his input was limited to seemingly unheeded, private communications with a few executive officials. Referring to those months, Richard Perle, a key Jackson aide on national security affairs, has commented that "Kissinger never felt a responsibility to engage in what you might call 'real consultation.'"[44]

On May 26, 1972, President Nixon and Secretary Brezhnev signed the SALT I accords in Moscow. The concluded agreements dealt with both offensive and defensive weapons. The final maneuverings within the U.S. government to achieve a unified position, the frantic last-minute negotiations between President Nixon and General Secretary Brezhnev, the actual details of the initialed agreements--these were virtually unknown to the Congress and the American people. Despite public rhetoric to the contrary, the executive branch had completely dominated U.S. policy-making for SALT I and had, in fact, purposefully prevented Congress from overseeing or providing any substantive influence on the U.S. negotiating posture at the SALT talks. In its turn, the Congress, save for the efforts of a few individual senators, notably Cooper and Jackson, passively acquiesced in executive dominance over SALT policy issues and gave the Nixon administration virtually unquestioned support for its policies.

After the actual conclusion of the SALT I accord, this situation changed. The agreement to limit ABMs was concluded in treaty form and required Senate ratification, and the Interim Agreement on Offensive Weapons was concluded as an executive agreement and had to be approved by a simple majority of both Houses of Congress, according to the 1961 legislation that created the Arms Control and Disarmament Agency. This statute, the impetus for which came from the House of Representatives, provided:

> ...no action shall be taken under this or any law that will obligate the United States to disarm or to reduce or to limit the Armed Forces or armaments of the United States, except pursuant to the treaty-making power of the President under the Constitution or unless authorized by further affirmative legislation by the Congress of the United States.[45]

Accordingly, it behooved the Nixon administration to work closely with Congress in the period immediately following the conclusion of SALT I. Congress, for its part, had no choice but to be actively involved in the process by which the SALT agreements were approved and enacted into law.

Concerned about potential congressional criticism of the accords signed in Moscow, self-consciously anxious not to repeat Woodrow Wilson's unfortunate experience with Congress regarding the League of Nations, and believing that SALT and detente could help him in his upcoming re-election campaign, President Nixon undertook a series of steps to minimize the possibility of congressional rejection of the SALT I accords. First, the administration endeavored in good faith to explain to Congress the substance of the accords. On the day before the agreements were signed in Moscow, Richard Perle and Dorothy Fosdick of Senator Jackson's staff and George Will of Senator Gordon Allott's staff were invited to the White House for a briefing on the agreements. The three Senate aides met with Philip Odeen and John Lehman of the National Security Council staff and discussed for more than three hours the details of the proposed agreements.[46]

Within thirty minutes of his return to Washington from Moscow on June 1, President Nixon took the unusual step of addressing a joint session of Congress on SALT. The president explained in the nationally televised address that in the agreement both sides renounced the option of a nationwide ABM system and agreed to limit ABM deployments to two sites. Numbers of strategic offensive missile launchers were to be frozen as of July 1, 1972. The United States could have 1,054 ICBMs and no more than 710 SLBM launchers, while the Soviets could have 1,618 ICBMs and 740 SLBM launchers and could convert up to 210 of their old ICBMs to SLBM launchers. Strategic bombers, an area in which the United States enjoyed a significant advantage, were not covered by the five-year Interim Agreement. Also, no restrictions were placed on MIRVs, forward-based systems, or land-based mobile ICBMs, although it was commonly understood that some of these would be among the issues to be negotiated in subsequent SALT negotiations.[47]

In his remarks to the joint session, Nixon urged speedy action on the Treaty and Interim Agreement, suggesting that ratification would "forestall a major spiralling of the arms race." Nixon also expressed the hope that the legislative branch would examine both agreements closely, declaring that "the fullest national scrutiny" would underscore the fact that these accords are "in the interest of both nations." Finally, the president made it clear that administration officials would be willing to spend virtually as much time briefing Congress as necessary to clarify the nature of the SALT I accords.[48]

In this, Nixon was true to his word. On June 15, the president and Henry Kissinger spent more than two hours in the White House briefing some 120 senators and representatives on the details of the agreements. At one point, Nixon noted that Kissinger would not be able to testify before Congress in behalf of the agreements for reasons of executive privilege. "However," Nixon added:

> ...since this is really an unprecedented situation, it seemed to me that it was important that he appear before the members in this format. This is on the record.... What we are asking for here...is cooperation and not just rubber-stamping by the House and the Senate. That is essential because there must be follow-through on this and the members of the House and Senate, it seems to me, must be convinced that they played a role as they have up to this point, and will continue to play a role in this very, very important field of arms control.[49]

In his substantive remarks at the June 15 briefing, Nixon emphasized that the agreements had been "toughly negotiated on both sides," and that "neither side won and neither side lost." Nixon then remarked, "I have noted a great deal of speculation about these negotiations. As a matter of fact, if we were to really look at it very, very fairly, both sides won, and the whole world won."[50]

In Kissinger's remarks, which followed those of the president, the rationale for and details of the SALT I accords were comprehensively spelled out in a way that had not taken place previously. At one point during the question-and-answer period with Kissinger, Senator Claiborne Pell, a senior member of the Foreign Relations Committee, revealingly inquired of the presidential assistant: "Why, in this set of negotiations, was the constitutionally normal course of Congressional consultation, advice as well as consent, not engaged in?" To this query, Kissinger had no good answer. In reply, he lamely noted: "As for the process of consultation, this is not my specialty, but it has been my understanding that Mr. Smith and the appropriate Secretaries have been in close consultation and we have tried from here to be...in contact with key Senators."[51]

Reiterating many of the same points that President Nixon and Kissinger had made in their June 15 White House briefings, Secretary of State Rogers, Secretary of Defense Laird, SALT negotiator Smith, and several other administration witnesses subsequently testified at length on the SALT accords before the Senate Foreign Relations Committee.[52] Similarly, in June-July 1972, Secretary Laird; Ambassador Smith; Thomas Moorer, Chairman of the Joint Chiefs of Staff; Paul Nitze, Assistant to the Secretary of Defense for SALT; and others testified before the Senate Armed Services Committee on SALT.[53] In short, administration witnesses had never been so available to testify before Congress on U.S. strategic arms policy as they were during the weeks immediately following the signing of the accords in Moscow when the Congress was considering the ratification of the initialed documents.

A second step the Nixon administration took to minimize the possibility that Congress might not ratify the SALT agreements was to link the accords with an aggressive weapons modernization program within the constraints of the agreements. Secretary Laird, Admiral Moorer, and several influential members of the Senate Armed Services Committee (e.g., Stennis, Jackson, Tower, Thurmond) were concerned that American adherence to the Interim Agreement on Offensive Weapons might well leave the United States in 1977 in an inferior position vis-a-vis the Soviet Union. To preempt potential congressional opposition as well as to achieve a unified administration position in support of the SALT accords, Secretary Laird--presumably with President Nixon's approval--argued in favor of ratification of the SALT accords but linked it with approval of additional funds to accelerate, among other things, the Trident submarine, the B-1 bomber, and the strategic cruise missile.[54] On June 20, 1972, in testimony on the SALT I accords before the Senate Armed Services Committee, Laird noted that as Secretary of Defense he could not support the SALT I agreements "without the assurance that these follow-on programs [Trident, B-1, strategic cruise missile] would go forward," and declared, "I would certainly recommend that we not go forward with this agreement or this treaty if we are going to abandon the programs that have been outlined in the strategic weapons field."[55] For Laird, these additional monies were, on the one hand, potential bargaining chips in future SALT negotiations with the Soviets. On the other hand, they were essential in the short run to America's maintenance of its "technical superiority" over the Soviet Union. In this regard, the Secretary of Defense, in his testimony before

Congress, did not hesitate to mention Chairman Brezhnev's admission to President Nixon in Moscow that the Soviet Union planned to go ahead with those offensive weapons programs not covered by the strategic arms limitation accords.[56]

Because of the linkage issue, it was of some consequence whether the Senate vote on the ratification of the SALT I accords preceded or followed the vote on the Fiscal Year 1973 Military Procurement Authorization Bill, the legislation that contained additional monies for Trident, B-1, and cruise missile development. If the vote on the SALT agreements came first, then they would presumably be considered on their own merits, rather than being held hostage to the authorization for additional monies. Despite Kissinger's hint to congressional leaders that the two items be considered separately, each on its own merits,[57] the administration tacitly engineered consideration of the authorization bill first. Amendments to the legislation to delete the supplementary monies for Trident and B-1 were subsequently defeated, and on August 2 the authorization bill passed the Senate by a vote of 92-5.[58]

On the very next day, the ABM treaty was brought up on the Senate floor for a vote. Discussion of the agreement was limited. The prevailing mood was indifference. At one point Senate Majority Leader Mansfield, disappointed by the lack of more senatorial interest in the treaty, declared:

> We are considering one of the most important treaties... to come before this body in a good many years. There seems little or no interest...on the part of the membership to discuss the pending business.... We will just have to stand twiddling our thumbs, and wait for the expiration of the time limitation, unless those who wish to offer amendments or understandings, or those who wish to speak on this most important treaty, will come to the floor and undertake the responsibilities which are theirs and which are the Senate's collectively.[59]

Few senators responded to Mansfield's call. And after a remarkably short couple of hours of debate, given the significance of the subject, the Senate ratified the ABM Treaty by a vote of 88-2.[60]

Following the Senate's *pro forma* handling of the ABM Treaty, the administration pressed for an early vote on the Interim Agreement to Limit Offensive Weapons. Since the Foreign Relations Committee had approved ratifying legislation without dissent, there was hope within the administration that the Interim Agreement would be ratified as expeditiously as the ABM Treaty.

This hope was to be short-lived, however. On August 3, the same day the Senate approved the ABM Treaty, a group of senators let it be known that they intended to offer a series of amendments to the resolution ratifying the Interim Agreement when that legislation was called up on the Senate floor. Surprisingly, this group, led by Senator Henry Jackson, claimed that the administration was backing its efforts.[61]

In the weeks following President Nixon's return from Moscow on June 1, Senator Jackson assiduously used the Armed Services Committee hearings on the military implications of the SALT I accords to build a case against the Interim Agreement. In these hearings and through the media, Senator Jackson made known in detail his views about why the Interim Agreement raised "some very serious questions that go to the heart of the security of the United States and the future of individual liberty."[62] What troubled Jackson and like-minded senators about the Interim Agreement was the accord's condition that froze the United States at a serious numerical inferiority in both ICBMs and SLBMs and left the Soviets free to develop MIRVs. Jackson feared that if the Interim Agreement was ratified as initially drawn up, the Soviet Union would have a significant advantage in terms of throw-weight and might well develop a first-strike capability during the five-year duration of the accord.[63] Given America's "interim sub-parity," Jackson reasoned that this might lead the Soviet Union to attack the Atlantic Alliance's forward-based systems in Central Europe or even "intervene militarily in the affairs of China."[64]

In the Armed Services Committee hearings, Jackson vigorously criticized not only the substantive content of the agreements, but also the administration's handling of SALT I vis-à-vis Congress. At different times in the hearings, Senator Jackson admonished administration witnesses for not being more "forthcoming" with Congress on SALT issues; for selectively declassifying information concerning its key assertions; for hiding from Congress "relevant" negotiating details and aide-memoires; for concluding "secret misunderstandings" in Moscow; and, in general, for being too eager to conclude a SALT agreement and therefore not "levelling" with Congress on the "real" meaning of the accords that were signed.[65]

To prevent what he perceived to be the mistakes of SALT I--both substantive and procedural--from being repeated in subsequent SALT negotiations, Senator Jackson decided to try to amend the legislation ratifying the Interim Agreement. What Jackson and others wanted to do was provide "advisory language which would be a matter of policy guidance from the Congress" for subsequent strategic arms talks.[66]

Jackson's proposed amendment to the Interim Agreement, which would be advisory rather than binding in its effect, called for numerical equality in future strategic arms agreements, something which the Soviets had, in fact, insisted on in the ABM Treaty. Equality was to refer to the numbers of ICBMs and SLBMs each side had--something that was covered in the Interim Agreement--and also to the number of strategic bombers, which was not included in the SALT I agreement. Equality was also to imply a rough balance between the two sides in terms of throw-weight, but it was not to include America's strategic systems based in Europe.

In addition to calling for equality, the Jackson amendment put the Soviet Union on notice that, pending the conclusion of a permanent agreement to limit offensive systems, the United States would view Russian deployments threatening America's deterrent forces as contrary to this country's supreme national interest. Of particular concern here was potential Soviet development of a hard-target MIRV capability for their large SS-9 missiles. Finally, the Jackson amendment called for "the maintenance of a vigorous research and development program" in support of a "prudent strategic posture."[67]

Before deciding to introduce such legislation, Senator Jackson went to see President Nixon at the White House. Jackson explained to the president his misgivings about the Interim Agreement and talked about his proposed amendment. President Nixon agreed with the basic principles underlying the proposed amending legislation and assured Senator Jackson of his support. The president, according to one account, then said concerning the amendment, "I am with you all the way through."[68] Thus the Nixon administration, in backing the Jackson Amendment to the Interim Agreement, had taken a third key step in its efforts to ensure congressional ratification of the SALT I accords.

During the afternoon of August 3, Jackson circulated a copy of the proposed amendment to his colleagues in the Senate. Jackson invited co-sponsors to join this initiative, indicating that his efforts had the support of the White House. Several senators, including Minority Leader Hugh Scott, quickly agreed to co-sponsor the amendment. However, a few members of the Foreign Relations Committee, which the day before had unanimously approved without amendment ratifying legislation to the Interim Agreement, were perplexed by the administration's seeming support of the Jackson amendment. Committee Chairman Fulbright, upon reading about the proposed amendment in the August 3 New York Times, remarked on the Senate floor:

> The committee [Foreign Relations Committee] acted unanimously...to report both the treaty and interim agreement, without encumbering reservations or understandings of any kind. It was my understanding at the time that this was in accord with the desires of the administration.... I was not at all taken aback by the fact that Senator Jackson anticipated offering or was going to offer criticisms or reservations or anything else....
> [What] bothers me and concerns me is that this is with administration support.[69]

Fulbright added that without administration support, Jackson would not "get anywhere."[70]

In response to inquiries from Fulbright, several other senators, and the media, the White House publicly announced late on August 3 that it was "not pushing" the Jackson amendment but that the legislation was "consistent with U.S. policy."[71] A White House official, attempting to shed some light on the rationale behind the announcement, explained that the administration desired to use the Jackson amendment as an indication of a tough congressional attitude to increase its bargaining leverage at the next round of strategic arms negotiations.[72] One subsequent press report noted that the administration felt it needed Senator Jackson's support in order to ensure ratification of the Interim Agreement and acceptance of the amendment was the price of the Washington senator's backing. It added, "for the White House, Jackson's support was important in overcoming reservations among conservatives [in Congress] about an agreement that conferred a numerical superiority in offensive weapons on the Soviet Union."[73]

Over the weekend of August 5-6, John Lehman of the National Security Council staff met with Richard Perle of Senator Jackson's staff to discuss further the proposed amending legislation. Henry Kissinger had been under severe pressure from the Soviets to try to modify the original wording of the amendment. Two points were of particular concern to the Soviet government as well as to much of the SALT bureaucracy within the executive branch--the language concerning equality and the suggestion that a perceived Soviet threat against the survivability of U.S. land-based forces would trigger American withdrawal from the Interim Agreement.

Perle and, ultimately, Senator Jackson, believing that White House support was necessary for congressional passage of the amendment, acceded to the administration's wishes to change the language of the amendment. The clause concerning possible U.S. withdrawal from the Agreement, which some officials at the State Department felt was an insulting threat to the Soviet Union, was eliminated. The modified language read, "were the survivability of the strategic deterrent forces of the United States to be threatened, this <u>could</u> jeopardize the supreme national interests of the United States."[74] Concerning numerical equality, the initial wording of the Jackson amendment was replaced by language requesting the president "to seek a future treaty that, <u>inter alia</u>, would not limit the United States to levels of intercontinental strategic forces inferior to the limits provided for the Soviet Union."[75]

With these changes agreed to, the White House announced on August 7 that it fully supported the Jackson amendment.[76] In the weeks that followed, however, several senators--notably Fulbright, Muskie, and Symington--attempted unsuccessfully to change the intent of the amendment. Other senators opted with little success to dilute the effect of the Jackson amendment by adding language of their own to the ratifying legislation. Senate Majority Leader Mansfield, for example, added an amendment to the legislation that explicitly incorporated portions of the May 20, 1972 Nixon-Brezhnev Declaration of Basic Principles of Mutual Relations. Senators Hughes and Brooke added an amendment which noted that neither side should seek unilateral advantage by developing a first-strike potential. However, on September 14, after several weeks of frequently acrimonious debate, the Senate passed, in essence, the White House-revised, August 7 version of the Jackson amendment by a vote of 56-35, and then ratified the Interim Agreement by a vote of 88-2.[77] After a one-hour debate, the House had earlier passed legislation ratifying the Interim Agreement, 329-7. Finally, on September 30, the president signed the Interim Agreement in an elaborate White House ceremony attended by several congressional leaders.

Following the signing ceremony, President Nixon and Senator Jackson conferred alone in the Rose Garden for some forty minutes. According to one account,[78] Senator Jackson made clear his dissatisfaction with the SALT negotiating effort and the "soft-headed" leadership of the Arms Control and Disarmament Agency. Further, Jackson expressed the opinion that the leadership of the SALT delegation and ACDA should be separated in the future and urged the president to install a new negotiating team for the next round of SALT, scheduled to begin in Geneva soon thereafter. In these judgments, the president concurred.[79]

Soon after his re-election in November 1972 President Nixon asked for the resignations of all appointed officials in the executive branch. In some agencies, the resignations were submitted and subsequently rejected. However, at the Arms Control and Disarmament Agency, the resignations of virtually all the top officials were accepted. In an earlier private conversation with the president, Gerard Smith had made known his intention to leave government service after SALT I was ratified. But several of Smith's chief assistants were, in fact, "purged" from the leadership ranks of ACDA. SALT I participant Joseph Kruzel explained soon thereafter, "It is a poorly kept secret in Washington that a mini-purge was conducted by the White House, at Senator Jackson's urging, in a deliberate attempt to start SALT II with a new team of officials unsullied by association with SALT I."[80]

Additionally, on January 4, 1973, the White House officially announced that the directorship of ACDA would henceforth be divorced from the chief SALT negotiator position, and U. Alexis Johnson, a career Foreign Service Officer, was picked to be the new head of the U.S. SALT delegation. A few months later, Fred Iklé, a Rand Corporation analyst who had previously written studies for Senator Jackson's Government Operations Subcommittee on National Security Affairs, was appointed director of ACDA. Seemingly, Senator Jackson had not only played a central role in providing "advisory language" to the U.S. negotiators for SALT II, but also had institutionalized some of his criticism of how the first round of SALT had been conducted.

A SUMMING UP

Overall, the Senate did not play a very meaningful role in the formulation of U.S. policy during SALT I. During the two and one-half years that the strategic arms limitation agreements were being negotiated, the executive branch exercised a dominant influence on the policy process, while the Senate was by and large content to acquiesce in and support executive branch initiatives. Specifically, during the period November 1969-May 1972, neither the Senate as an institution, nor its constituent committees or subcommittees, nor the overwhelming majority of individual members: (1) kept closely informed about the U.S. position at SALT and the details of the issues under negotiation; (2) pressed administration officials to explain or defend U.S. SALT policies; (3) questioned or debated the executive's goals at SALT or the underlying bases for the U.S. negotiating positions; (4) built much public support for or broadened the terms of the debate on American SALT policy; (5) developed alternative policies to those of the executive branch, except concerning limiting the deployment of ABMs and MIRVs and then only belatedly with very limited effect; (6) participated in setting the general directions of U.S. SALT policy; or (7) held key executive officials accountable for American policies.

To be sure, certain individual senators such as John Sherman Cooper of Kentucky and Henry Jackson of Washington tried to oversee and become involved in the U.S. SALT policy process. But even their efforts, which were notably different from those of their congressional colleagues, were of a sporadic nature and of limited consequence vis-à-vis SALT policy.

To some extent, the pattern of executive-legislative relations concerning U.S. SALT policy changed immediately following the successful conclusion of the SALT I accords in May 1972. Following the Moscow summit, the Nixon administration undertook at least three steps to ensure ratification of the agreed-upon accords. First, the administration during the summer of 1972 endeavored to consult closely and frequently with Congress, responsible congressional committees and interested individual senators and representatives on the substantive content of the accords. Second, the administration agreed to link approval of the SALT agreements with an aggressive offensive weapons modernization program to appease potential conservative criticism in Congress. And third, the administration opted to back the Jackson amendment to the

Interim Offensive Weapons Agreement, a move designed to preempt possible criticism from those members of the Senate unhappy with the numerical disparities contained in the accord.

In its turn, Congress ratified the SALT I agreements, but not before the Senate discussed, debated, and amended the Interim Agreement. In the end, the resolution approving the agreement bore the imprint of several senators, most notably Jackson, who added significant, substantive language to the ratifying legislation.

Even here, though, the role of the Senate should not be overstated. For the amendment which Jackson added to the legislation ratifying the Interim Agreement provided guidelines for SALT II, not SALT I, and had been, in fact, rewritten by the National Security Council staff. In addition, both this legislation and the post-SALT I personnel shifts in the U.S. SALT negotiating team and ACDA, which were at least partially inspired by congressional unhappiness over the SALT I accords, did have the personal support of the president.

Was the Senate's role in SALT II during the 1972-76 years different from that in SALT I? That is the central concern of the next chapter.

NOTES

1. The New York Times (hereafter NYT) November 13, 1969.
2. The Washington Post (hereafter WP), November 13, 1969.
3. Ibid., November 14, 1969.
4. NYT, November 14, 1969.
5. Curiously, Gerard Smith stopped in Brussels en route to Helsinki to brief the NATO Council on U.S. thinking about SALT. In A Responsible Congress, Alton Frye, an aide to Senate Armed Services Committee member Edward Brooke during the 1969-71 years, has revealingly noted: "It is fair to say that the leaders of Congress and the relevant committees received less detailed and substantive exchange on SALT than did the allied governments of the North Atlantic Treaty Organization, which were regularly briefed at length prior to each session of the negotiations." P. 84.
6. Cold Dawn: The Story of SALT (New York: Holt, Rinehart and Winston, 1973), p. 159.
7. White House Press Briefing by Henry Kissinger, June 15, 1972, White House Press Release, June 15, 1972. For further discussions of the Verification Panel and its role in SALT, see President Nixon's Annual Report to the Congress, February 25, 1971, pp. 188-89.
8. See Graham Allison, An Overview to the Commission on the Organization of the Government for the Conduct of Foreign Policy (Washington: Government Printing Office, 1975), pp. 76-79. For a detailed discussion of how the executive branch

organized for SALT I, see Bert Rosenthal, "Formulating Negotiating Positions for SALT: 1968, 1969-72," Report of the Commission on the Organization of Foreign Policy, Vol. 4, Part V, Section 3, pp. 325-48. See also Roger Morris, Uncertain Greatness: Henry Kissinger and American Foreign Policy (New York: Harper and Row, 1977), pp. 208-212.

9. "Hearings on International Negotiations" before the Subcommittee on National Security and International Operations, Committee on Government Operations, U.S. Senate, 92nd Congress, 2d Session, July 25, 1972, p. 221.

10. For further discussion of the "building blocks" approach to SALT, see Newhouse, pp. 170-71.

11. Newhouse, p. 172.

12. Henry Brandon, The Retreat of Power (Garden City: Doubleday, 1973), pp. 309-10.

13. Newhouse, p. 182.

14. Ibid.

15. Some have suggested that the Nixon administration was not prepared to accept a moratorium on MIRV testing in 1970 and hence proposed a MIRV ban policed by on-site inspectors, knowing full well that the Soviets would not agree to this. See, for example, Desmond Ball, Déja Vu: The Return to Counterforce in the Nixon Administration, Southern California Seminar on Arms Control (December 1974), p. 19. Newhouse has summarized Soviet thinking about on-site inspection as follows: "The Soviets strenuously oppose on-site inspection, partly because it is intrusive; partly because of an understandable aversion to parading their technological inferiority vis-à-vis the United States; partly because they suspect Americans of seeking targeting information not otherwise available or just wanting to pry, and perhaps partly of a concern that to disclose one thing could mean disclosing other things they prefer to keep secret." Newhouse, p. 180.

16. Lawrence Weiler, a member of the U.S. SALT delegation, has persuasively argued that Congress and the American people never knew the real nature of the initial U.S. MIRV proposal and that the executive branch was content throughout 1970 to have Congress believe that the SALT negotiators were still pursuing a ban on MIRVs, when, in fact, this American proposal was dropped in July 1970, after only two months of actual negotiations. Weiler is of the opinion that had Congress been kept accurately informed on the U.S. negotiating position, a MIRV ban might have been agreed to at SALT I. See Lawrence Weiler, The Arms Race, Secret Negotiations and the Congress, Occasional Paper #12, The Stanley Foundation (1976), pp. 18-21.

17. "Statement of the Secretary of the Air Force Robert Seamans on the Fiscal Year 1971 Authorizations for Military Procurement, Research and Development and Reserve Strength." Committee on Armed Services, U.S. Senate, 91st Congress, 2d Session, Part 2 (Washington: Government Printing Office,

1970), p. 907.

18. "ABM, MIRV, SALT and the Nuclear Arms Race," p. 9. For a detailed discussion of the reasons for initial Senate inaction on Senate Resolution 211, see Alton Frye, A Responsible Congress, pp. 55-71.

19. Frye, p. 72.

20. WP, March 22, 1970, p. A-1. It should be noted that this resolution expressed a viewpoint similar to the position that the Arms Control and Disarmament Agency was espousing within the executive branch, a position that was not adopted by the administration. Confidential Interview.

21. Thomas Dine, "The Issue of Arms Control in the Senate Foreign Relations Committee." (Unpublished paper, Harvard University, June 30, 1975), p. 66.

22. "Hearings on International Negotiation" before the Subcommittee on National Security and International Operations of the Committee on Government Operations, U.S. Senate, p. 203.

23. Senate Executive Report 92-28, July 21, 1972, p. 2.

24. Frye, A Responsible Congress, p. 73.

25. Bernard Kalb and Marvin Kalb, Kissinger (Boston: Little, Brown and Co., 1974), p. 118. Kissinger's assumption in the summer of 1970 that the Soviets would not agree to a moratorium on MIRVs was not universally shared. Lawrence Weiler, a member of the U.S. SALT delegation at the time, holds that had the United States put forward a serious MIRV proposal in 1970, the Soviets might well have responded positively to the American proposal. Weiler, p. 21. For further support of this view, see William Beecher, "Soviet Diplomats Hint Interest in MIRV Curbs," NYT, March 12, 1970. For a general discussion of Soviet thinking about limiting MIRVs, see Ted Greenwood, Making the MIRV: A Study of Defense Decision Making (Cambridge: Ballinger Publishing Co., 1975), pp. 133-34.

26. Ibid. Newhouse, p. 186.

27. WP, March 24, 1970.

28. Dine, p. 64.

29. WP, March 24, 1970.

30. There was, moreover, significant congressional debate in 1975 as to whether or not to close down the one U.S. ABM site at Grand Forks. In the end, led by Senator Edward Kennedy, Congress decided to close the site. See Congressional Record, November 14, 1975, pp. S20139-46.

31. "The Foreign Policy of President Nixon: A Vote of Confidence." Speech before the World Affairs Council of Boston, August 17, 1971.

32. Newhouse, pp. 203-4.

33. See Marquis Childs, WP, June 1, 1971.

34. NYT, May 21, 1971.

35. Congressional Record, June 14, 1971, p. 24992.

36. Greenwood, pp. 134, 138. It should be noted that there was one change in the U.S. MIRV program in 1971 that resulted from congressional criticism of the program: the can-

cellation of stellar inertial guidance for Poseidon. In the course of arguing for a MIRV escrow amendment, Senator Humphrey had argued at length about the wisdom of limiting the capability of American MIRVs to destroy Soviet missile silos. The stellar inertial guidance system was part of this capability, and after the debate on the Humphrey amendment, the administration decided to drop the system. However, it is not entirely certain that the decision to drop the stellar inertial guidance system was the direct result of Humphrey's anti-MIRV deployment arguments. For the decision to forego the system was made during a Defense Department budget review meeting, the purpose of which was to prune the outlays of the Pentagon. In addition, the Special Projects Office of the Defense Department was not all that supportive of this particular system at any time. Greenwood, pp. 135-36.

37. Although 1971 ended in a virtual U.S.-Soviet stalemate on offensive weapons limitations, two collateral agreements were signed in the Fall of 1971: (1) a plan to modernize the hot line between Moscow and Washington by using satellites to insure quick and reliable communication during crises and (2) an understanding on procedures to reduce the risk of accidental or unintended nuclear war. NYT, October 1, 1971. For a detailed discussion of the various SALT proposals considered in Washington and ultimately tabled by our negotiating team during the May 1971-May 1972 period, see Newhouse, pp. 219-49.

38. For a revealing discussion of senatorial thinking in 1969-72 about the desirability of active congressional involvement in SALT in particular and national security matters in general, see the 1970 debate that took place on the Senate floor regarding Senate Resolution 211. Congressional Record, April 9, 1970, pp. 11045-57.

39. Interview with John Sherman Cooper, April 16, 1975.

40. Confidential Interview.

41. In January 1973, this subcommittee became known as the Government Operations Subcommittee on Permanent Investigations.

42. Confidential Interview.

43. Peter Ognibene, Scoop: The Life and Politics of Henry M. Jackson (New York: Stein and Day, 1975), pp. 202-3.

44. Interview with Richard Perle, July 28, 1976. See also Frye, pp. 85-86.

45. United States Statutes at Large, 87th Congress, 1st Session, 1961, Vol. 75 (Washington: GPO, 1961), p. 631.

46. Interview with John Lehman, July 27, 1976, and with Richard Perle, July 28, 1976.

47. The ABM treaty, the Interim Agreement on Offensive Weapons, and the Protocol to the Interim Agreement are reprinted in Arms Control and Disarmament Agreements: Texts and History of Negotiations (Washington: Government Printing Office, 1975), pp. 133-49.

48. NYT, June 2, 1972.
49. "Remarks of the President at a Congressional Briefing on the Arms Limitation Treaty and Agreement, June 15, 1972," reprinted in "Hearings on the Military Implications of the Treaty on the Limitations of Anti-Ballistic Missile Systems and the Interim Agreement on Limitation of Strategic Offensive Arms" before the Committee on Armed Services, U.S. Senate, 92nd Congress, 2d Session, June-July 1972 (Washington: Government Printing Office, 1972), p. 114.
50. Ibid.
51. "The White House, Question and Answer Session After a Briefing by Dr. Henry Kissinger, Assistant to the President for National Security Affairs," reprinted in "Hearings on the Military Implications of the Treaty on the Limitations of Anti-Ballistic Missile Systems....," p. 135.
52. See "Hearings on the Strategic Arms Limitation Agreements before the Committee on Foreign Relations," United States Senate, 92nd Congress, 2d Session, June-July 1972 (Washington: Government Printing Office, 1972).
53. See "Hearings on the Military Implications of the Treaty on the Limitations of the Anti-Ballistic Missile Systems..."
54. On this question of linkage between the SALT I agreements and the Trident and B-1 weapons requests, there is some confusion concerning the president's position. In the June 15 congressional briefing at the White House, President Nixon endorsed the linkage. At the same time, at a June 22 press conference, the president endorsed the idea that the accords were justified on their merits. For discussion of this linkage, see Jonathan Medalia,"The U.S. Senate and Strategic Arms Limitation Policymaking, 1963-1972" (Ph.D. Dissertation, Stanford University, 1975), pp. 155-56. Also, see John Steinbruner and Barry Carter, "Organizational and Political Dimensions of the Strategic Posture: The Problems of Reform," Daedalus (Summer 1975): 140-41.
55. "Hearings on the Military Implications of the Treaty on the Limitations of Anti-Ballistic Missile Systems...," pp. 151-52.
56. Ibid., pp. 29-30.
57. See "The White House, Question and Answer Session After a Briefing by Dr. Henry Kissinger," reprinted in 'Hearings...," p. 125.
58. For a more detailed discussion of the linkage issue, see Medalia, pp. 155-59. Also, see Kurt Lauk, "Possibilities of Senatorial Influence: The Case of the Jackson Amendment to SALT I" (unpublished paper, Stanford University, June 1975), pp. 10-14.
59. Congressional Record, August 3, 1972, p. 26684.
60. Only Senators Buckley and Allen voted against the ABM Treaty. For the Senate debate on the ABM Treaty, see Congressional Record, August 3, 1972, pp. 26678-710, 26762-70.

61. See NYT, August 3, 1972.
62. Henry Jackson, "Weapons Agreements: A Senator Questions U.S. Concessions," Los Angeles Times, June 25, 1972.
63. "Hearing on the Military Implications of the Treaty on the Limitations of Anti-Ballistic Missile Systems...," p. 415.
64. Ibid., p. 370.
65. Ibid., pp. 296-305, 310-11, 407-408, 581-92.
66. Ibid., p. 407.
67. The full text of the Jackson Amendment is reprinted in Strategic Arms Limitation Talks (SALT): Legislative History of the Jackson Amendment, 1972. This document, compiled by Richard Perle of Senator Jackson's staff, includes the full record of Senate and House consideration of the Jackson Amendment. The final language of the amendment appears on pp. i-ii.
68. Lauk, p. 27n. At least one newspaper report at the time suggested that Senator Jackson had succeeded in getting President Nixon's written support for the amendment. NYT, August 5, 1972.
69. Strategic Arms Limitation Talks: Legislative History of the Jackson Amendment, 1972, p. 3.
70. Ibid.
71. WP, August 4, 1972.
72. NYT, August 5, 1972.
73. Ibid., August 10, 1972.
74. Strategic Arms Limitation Talks: Legislative History of the Jackson Amendment, 1972, pp. 128-29.
75. Ibid.
76. See NYT, August 8, 1972.
77. See Strategic Arms Limitation Talks: Legislative History of the Jackson Amendment, 1972, pp. 153-219.
78. Ognibene, pp. 210-14.
79. Confid. Interview. Ognibene, pp. 210-14. At this September 30, 1972 meeting with President Nixon in the Rose Garden, Senator Jackson also discussed the matter of Jewish emigration from the Soviet Union. Jackson agreed, however, not to bring this issue up in the course of the 1972 presidential campaign. See Paula Stern, "The Water's Edge: The Jackson Amendment as a Case Study of the Role Domestic Politics Plays in the Creation of American Foreign Policy" (Ph.D. dissertation, The Fletcher School of Law and Diplomacy, 1976), pp. 121-22.
80. Quoted in Congressional Quarterly, June 15, 1974, p. 1546. It should be noted that Richard Perle of Senator Jackson's staff disclaims any role for himself or his boss in the 1972 "purging" of ACDA. Interview with Richard Perle, July 28, 1976.

3. SALT II, 1972-1976

In October 1972, virtually three years after SALT I had begun, the United States and the Soviet Union formally implemented the strategic arms limitation agreements. The following month the next round of negotiations, SALT II, began in Geneva. This set of talks was to take up, in President Nixon's words, "those new issues inherent in working out permanent, rather than temporary, arrangements and some of the problems set aside in SALT I."[1] Among the most prominent problems not covered in the SALT I accords were: MIRVs, forward-based systems, mobile ICBMs, strategic bombers, cruise missiles, missile accuracies, throw-weight, anti-submarine warfare, and missile reductions. These were, in fact, the principal issues addressed at SALT II in the 1972-76 years.

The first session of SALT II began on November 21, 1972 and lasted only four weeks. During these talks, which were of a general, exploratory nature, neither side presented any formal proposals. The American delegation had no specific instructions nor, it seemed, did their Soviet counterparts. The Soviet delegation did, however, express a general interest in setting limits on MIRVs; this surprised the American delegation. For our negotiators were under the impression that the Soviets would not be willing to discuss MIRV restraints in the second round of SALT, given current U.S. deployments and the fact that the Soviets had not yet tested a MIRV. But the Soviet delegation did raise the MIRV issue at the same time as emphasizing the need to limit American forward-based systems in Europe. The sole concrete achievement of the first session of SALT II was the establishment of a four-person consultative commission. Called for in the SALT I accords, this commission was to supervise past and future agreements.

At the conclusion of the first round of SALT II in late December 1972, Gerard Smith officially announced that he would be leaving government service. Soon thereafter, President Nixon nominated U. Alexis Johnson to be the new head of the U.S. SALT delegation. Within four weeks of his nomination, Johnson was confirmed by the Senate Foreign Relations

Committee as chief SALT negotiator with the rank of ambassador. Despite 1) Johnson's lack of previous background in the arms control field, 2) the administration's decision in early 1973 to reduce ACDA's budget by one-third for Fiscal Year 1974, and 3) the lack of specific American proposals during the first round of SALT II, Johnson's January 31 confirmation hearing was pro forma. Some of the questioning focused on Johnson's health, for the nominee was sixty-four years old and had suffered a heart attack several months earlier. Most of the rest of the questioning concerned Indochina and the recently completed Vietnam peace accords in which Johnson, as Under Secretary of State for Political Affairs, had played a central role. When the matter of SALT II was raised, Johnson replied that he hoped to acquaint himself further with the specific matters involved in the negotiations before consulting with the committee. Furthermore, the chief SALT negotiator-designate expressed the view that if the Congress wanted to discuss strategic arms issues with him, it would best be done in closed session only. For, Johnson felt, SALT was not suitable for public discussion before the committee because of "the confidential nature of details."[2]

Besides being averse to testifying publicly on SALT matters, Johnson insisted that meetings with individual senators concerning strategic arms issues be strictly private. That is, no congressional staff members were to attend--no matter what their security clearance. Johnson felt that such privacy was essential if the classified material under discussion was to be effectively protected.[3]

Following Johnson's confirmation hearing and subsequent approval by the Foreign Relations Committee and the full Senate, Senators Muskie and Case, the chairman and ranking member respectively of the Foreign Relations Subcommittee on Arms Control, sought a subcommittee meeting with the new SALT negotiator prior to his departure for Geneva. The senators were particularly interested in exploring with Johnson both the precise role of ACDA in SALT II and Johnson's negotiating instructions for the second round of strategic arms talks.

On February 6, 1973, Muskie wrote a letter to OMB Director Roy Ash, inquiring about the proposed Fiscal Year 1974 ACDA budget cut and probing the administration's commitment to further arms control agreements following the successful conclusion of the SALT I accords and the re-election of President Nixon. In the letter to Ash, Muskie also inquired about "the precise role envisioned for ACDA in relation to SALT II." In reply, Ash indicated that he was unable to comment on this or several other SALT-related issues raised in the letter and noted that he had forwarded the letter to the Arms Control and Disarmament Agency. A few weeks later, Acting Director of ACDA Philip Farley sent Muskie a perfunctory response. Farley indicated that he was unable to comment on the specific questions concerning SALT that Muskie had raised but asserted that the Arms Control and Disarmament Agency would continue to play "an active role" in the SALT process.[4]

Given the administration's seeming lack of interest in arms control matters and the absence of a director at ACDA, Muskie felt that a closed door Arms Control Subcommittee meeting with Johnson was essential prior to the SALT negotiator's departure for Europe. However, no such hearing could be arranged, due to Johnson's "busy" schedule. Consequently, the new SALT negotiator left for Geneva in early March 1973 without ever discussing any of the specifics of SALT II in either public or private with the members of the Arms Control Subcommittee, the Foreign Relations Committee subcommittee charged with overseeing SALT, or with the Armed Services Subcommittee on SALT.

Soon thereafter, Muskie and Case sent a letter to Johnson, lamenting the fact that no Arms Control Subcommittee hearing could be arranged prior to the ambassador's departure. In the letter, the senators noted that "Members of the subcommittee will undoubtedly visit Geneva during sessions of the Strategic Arms Limitation Talks" and expressed the hope that Johnson would be "available on those occasions to discuss the progress of the negotiations." The letter concluded with an assurance to Johnson that "the subcommittee will be following the negotiations with great interest."[5]

A little more than two weeks later, Johnson responded to the Muskie-Case letter. He, too, lamented the fact that "it was not possible for us to arrange a meeting with the subcommittee prior to my departure." Johnson noted that he would be "happy" to meet with members of the subcommittee either in Geneva or upon his return to Washington. He added that in any case he would "seek to keep the subcommittee informed of significant developments."[6] This was to be, however, the last written communication between SALT negotiator Johnson and the Senate Subcommittee on Arms Control until the spring of 1975 when there was an exchange of communications prior to a trip to Europe by then Arms Control Subcommittee Chairman, Stuart Symington.

On March 19, 1973, the week after Johnson left for Geneva, fourteen House Republicans issued a report on the Strategic Arms Limitation Talks, "SALT II: Can the Arms Race be Ended?" Led by Representative William Whitehurst of Virginia, the congressional authors made it clear at the time the report was issued that they wished "to cooperate with the President, not criticize him."[7] However, as Whitehurst noted, the Republican congressmen--many of whom were members of the Foreign Affairs and Armed Services Committees--were concerned about the administration's seeming reliance on the bargaining-chip approach to SALT and wanted to put their concern on record. The representatives urged the Nixon administration to exercise "technological restraint" during the second round of SALT. Specifically, they exhorted the president not to make additional promises to the Pentagon to gain military support for future SALT agreements and argued that "the Administration should attempt to build on the confidence created by the first round [of SALT], instead of relying too heavily on the fear created by the threat of new deployments."[8]

In addition, the Republican representatives asserted that "no attempt should be made to tie the hands of U.S. negotiators by insisting on strict formulas of strategic parity." The report itself included statistics to refute the charge that the United States emerged second best from SALT I and to support the idea that the American and Soviet strategic nuclear arsenals were "roughly equal." The report also called for new initiatives in other areas of arms control and recommended an expanded role for Congress in the strategic arms area. In this last regard, the report urged that Congress "make a determined effort to link arms control issues to the defense budget." It noted, "Congressional committees concerned with defense spending should not only focus on fiscal and military issues, but these groups should also examine the implications of new programs for the prospects of future agreement at SALT II."[9]

Following the issuance of this report at a well-attended press conference, there was no follow-up by its congressional authors. Not surprisingly, the report was soon forgotten--both within the Congress and by the executive branch.

Three weeks later, on April 6, President Nixon formally nominated Fred Iklé to be the new Director of the Arms Control and Disarmament Agency. The directorship of ACDA had been vacant for more than three months, and the continuing vacancy had led some members of Congress to doubt the second Nixon administration's interest in a new arms control agreement.

Iklé's nomination to direct ACDA tended to heighten this doubt. Head of the Social Science Division at the Rand Corporation at the time of his appointment, Iklé had written an article in the January 1973 issue of Foreign Affairs which led many people inside and outside the Congress to question his commitment to the cause of arms control. In this article, "Can Deterrence Last Out the Century?", Iklé attacked several of the key tenets underpinning current U.S. deterrent theory and recommended a search for new weapons such as "smart bombs" that would "enable both sides to avoid the killing of vast millions and yet to inflict assured destruction on military, industrial, and transportation assets."[10]

Soon after the Iklé nomination, Amron Katz was nominated to be Assistant Director of ACDA for Science Technology, and Robert Behr was nominated to be Assistant Director of ACDA for Weapons Evaluation Control. Katz was an associate of Iklé's at Rand; Behr was a career military officer. Both men were known to be "hard-liners" toward the Soviet Union and skeptical of the SALT I accords. Not surprisingly, neither appointment did much to allay congressional concern about

Iklé's and the administration's commitment to the successful conclusion of a SALT II accord.

Accordigly, the confirmation hearings of Iklé, Katz, and Behr took on particular importance, for they seemed to offer the Senate an ideal opportunity (1) to explore the qualifications of the men nominated to lead the Arms Control and Disarmament Agency in the second Nixon administration, and (2) to probe the executive's thinking about SALT II. Arms Control Subcommittee Chairman Muskie seemed to recognize this opportunity when, on the day of the announcement of the Iklé nomination, he declared:

> In recent months, I have expressed serious doubts about the second Nixon Administration's commitment to arms control. I look forward to Mr. Ikle's confirmation hearings for two reasons. First, I look forward to hearing Mr. Ikle's views on the crucial arms control and military matters of today--SALT, MIRVs.... And I expect to give the Director-designate's ideas on these subjects very close scrutiny in light of his recent article in Foreign Affairs. Second, I look forward to hearing the Administration's views on arms control.[11]

The reaction of Senator William Fulbright to the Iklé nomination was quite different from that of Muskie. Fulbright was strongly opposed to the Jackson amendment to SALT I and was, in the spring of 1973, still upset at the administration's efforts in the summer of 1972 to appease conservatives in the Senate in order to gain support for the SALT I accords. Iklé's confirmation hearing was initially set for May 9. But Fulbright, as chairman of the Foreign Relations Committee, put the hearing off indefinitely. Senators Muskie and Humphrey objected. They felt that four months was long enough for ACDA to be leaderless and felt Iklé's confirmation hearing was a potentially valuable way to probe and influence the administration's views on arms control in general and SALT II in particular. In a May 10 letter to Senator Humphrey, Fulbright expressed reservations about the Iklé appointment, doubting that "Dr. Iklé would be inclined to rebuild the Agency which has been in the process of a post-election dismemberment by the very administration which now wishes to turn it over to Dr. Iklé." Fulbright added:

> After some early doubts and even some caustic questioning of its [ACDA's] research programs, I have in recent years come to believe the Agency is one of the few in the Government which have injected some new thinking into the bureaucratic channels of the Department of State and Defense.... [but] If the Agency is to have an inferior kind of relationship to State, Defense, and to the SALT negotiators, it might be better to abandon the Agency

altogether and in its place expand our own activities in the field.[12]

Humphrey answered the Fulbright letter on May 24. In reply, Humphrey expressed the hope that he and Muskie could "not only determine Iklé's fitness for the post, but also impress upon him and his colleagues our determination that this Agency not be downgraded." He added:

> ACDA desperately needs greater Congressional and public attention. If it is to be rejuvenated, I think Iklé's hearing will be the first step. I recommend that it take place in advance of Chairman Brezhnev's visit to the United States in order that we may impress upon Mr. Iklé our desire that his agency play an important role in the upcoming summit talks and related matters.... If there are any opportunities for a greater role for the Agency, they will only come at our Committee's insistence. I would hope that we may begin this process soon.[13]

Ultimately, Fulbright yielded and scheduled the Iklé confirmation hearing for June 13, 1973. Prior to the actual hearing, Iklé made "courtesy calls" to most of the members of the Foreign Relations Committee. In these private meetings, Iklé attempted to acquaint himself with both the members of the committee and their views on arms control. However, when matters of substance about SALT were raised, Iklé was general rather than specific and like Alexis Johnson, suggested that he would be in a better position to brief senators about strategic arms limitation matters after he was on the job for awhile.

At his confirmation hearing, Iklé's responses were similar to those he had given during his "courtesy calls"; if anything, the prospective ACDA director was even more circumspect at the public session than he had been in the private meetings. When the size of ACDA's budget was discussed, Iklé pledged to try to restore the Agency's annual authorization to the size it had been in the previous fiscal year. When asked about his commitment to the cause of arms control, Iklé's responses were perfunctorily reassuring. And when questioned about his recent article in <u>Foreign Affairs</u> and other substantive issues, such as the importance of limiting MIRVs and strategic bombers in SALT II, Iklé was alternately evasive, noncommital and deferential. At one point, Iklé remarked that the suspension of MIRV deployments would be taken up on a forthcoming trip by Chairman Brezhnev to Washington. When pressed further on this point by committee members, Iklé declared that he preferred not to go into the matter any further at that time and noted that his observation was "based on newspaper stories, rather than personal contacts with the White House."[14] In short, the hearing provided little substantive insight into Iklé's--or the administration's-- thinking about SALT II.15

Given the continuing unavailability of Presidential Assistant Kissinger to testify before the Congress on U.S. strategic arms policy (or any other issue) due to executive privilege and the disinclination of Johnson and Iklé to discuss the specifics of SALT II at their respective confirmation hearings, the only real opportunities the Foreign Relations Committee had to discuss the second round of SALT with the executive branch during the winter-spring of 1973 were presented by Secretary of State Rogers' appearances before the committee on February 21 and April 30. On both occasions, however, SALT II was raised in a general way by committee members and both times when Rogers' responses were not forthcoming, the matter was immediately dropped. At the February 21, 1973 hearing, for example, the following dialogue took place between Chairman Fulbright and the Secretary of State:

Fulbright: Can you tell us anything about that [SALT] for the moment? Is there any progress being made? Is there any encouragement from the SALT talks?
Rogers: Well, as you know, we are about to start another phase of the SALT talks.
Fulbright: It has not started yet?
Rogers: It has not started yet.
Fulbright: Then I will not pursue that.16

At both the February 21 and April 30 hearings, Secretary Rogers focused his remarks on Indochina, the Middle East, and foreign aid--subjects with which he was most familiar and which seemed to him and the committee members to be most salient.

A similar situation characterized relations between the executive branch and the Senate Armed Services Committee during much of 1973. In this case the absence of meaningful legislative involvement in SALT matters resulted in part from the general lack of committee interest in the second round of strategic arms talks that were just beginning, in part from the administration's general reluctance to discuss the substance of SALT with Congress, and in part from the sheer turnover of top personnel at the Defense Department. In late 1972, as the first Nixon administration was coming to an end, Secretary of Defense Melvin Laird and Deputy Secretary of Defense Kenneth Rush announced their intention to leave the Pentagon. Named to replace them were Elliot Richardson, then Secretary of Health, Education, and Welfare, and William Clements, a Texas businessman. On January 9, 10, 11, and 12, 1973, Richardson and Clements testified at their respective confirmation hearings before the Armed Services Committee. On questions relating to SALT II, both witnesses gave general, pro forma replies. In essence, both men declared that the negotiations were "important" and both affirmed support for the SALT I accords, including the Jackson amendment.[17] Similarly, in June 1973, when James Schlesinger was named to be Secretary of Defense to replace Elliot Richardson, who was to become Attorney General, there was a perceptible reluctance on the part of the prospective Defense Secretary to answer questions relating to SALT matters in any detail.[18] Like Johnson and Iklé before the Foreign Relations Committee at their confirmation hearings, Schlesinger suggested that he would be in a better position to brief the Congress on U.S. strategic arms policy after he was on the job for awhile.

The fact is that up to this time there was for SALT only one administration official--Henry Kissinger--who was competent to discuss with Congress the substance of the strategic arms issues under negotiation. Kissinger's briefings of Congress on SALT matters took place only on those rare occasions when the president and his assistant decided it was useful for the White House to discuss certain national security matters with Congress--in the spring of 1970 when the administration feared that monies for the Safeguard system would be cut; in the summer of 1972 when the administration sought congressional ratification of the SALT I accords; and in June 1973, prior to Chairman Brezhnev's trip to the United States.

In accordance with the 1972 Nixon-Brezhnev understanding to hold annual summit meetings, Chairman Brezhnev came to Washington in mid-June 1973 for an official nine-day visit. In the administration's view, the summit was to be "a confirmation of the historic change in Soviet-American relations signalled by President Nixon's visit to the Soviet Union,"[19] and a step "to provide an impetus to the second phase of the strategic arms limitation talks."[20]

Brezhnev arrived in Washington on June 16. During the first few days of his visit, Nixon and Brezhnev concluded agreements on matters as diverse as agriculture, air travel, education, and oceanography. Then they turned their attention to arms control. On June 21, an agreement was to be signed concerning the limitation of strategic offensive weapons; on June 22, a second accord was to be signed by the two countries to avoid nuclear conflict with other nations. Immediately before the signing of the June 21 agreement, the leading members of the Senate and House Foreign Relations and Armed Services Committees were invited to the White House for a briefing. It consisted essentially of Presidential Assistant Kissinger's explaining the soon-to-be-initiated Agreement on the Prevention of Nuclear War and the "Basic Principles Agreement," which was to be the guideline for subsequent SALT II negotiations. To many Members of Congress, the ideas contained in the "Basic Principles Agreement" seemed to be but a restatement of the general principles which President Nixon had declared in his 1973 Foreign Policy Report when the president noted that a future SALT agreement would:

-establish an essential equivalence in strategic capabilities;

-maintain the survivability of strategic forces in light of known and potential technological capabilities;

-provide for the replacement and modernization of older systems without upsetting the strategic balance;

-be subject to adequate verification;

-leave the security of third parties undiminished.[21]

In truth, these principles were contained, in some cases verbatim, in the 1973 "Basic Principles" agreement. At the congressional briefing at the White House, Kissinger saw fit to emphasize that one of the principles mandated that future U.S.-Soviet negotiations be guided by "the recognition of each other's equal security interests" and that another stated that a SALT II agreement could include numerical and technological limits on strategic offensive weapons. Kissinger noted, perhaps most significantly, that in the June 21 agreement both sides pledged to accelerate the talks so that a permanent treaty could be reached by the end of 1974, instead of 1977 as implied in the SALT I accords.

Several Members of Congress wondered in private about what the two negotiating teams had been doing in Geneva since the beginning of SALT II in November 1972, given the general nature of the approved June 1973 guidelines. Some senators attending the White House briefing wondered why President Nixon and Kissinger had invited them to the White House at all, given the one-sided nature of the so-called "briefing" and the fact that the agreed-on principles had already been stated and were sufficiently general to be of little significance. Other senators wondered when the day would come when the executive branch would engage in "give-and-take" with Members of Congress concerning the details of the issues being negotiated in the second round of SALT--such matters as the status of the U.S. bomber force in Western Europe and the possibility for both sides to limit MIRVs (two matters neatly by-passed in the briefing and the agreement).

When President Nixon nominated Henry Kissinger to be Secretary of State in mid-August 1973, it appeared that the day of detailed consultation with the executive branch on strategic arms issues was close at hand. The nomination of Presidential Assistant Kissinger to be Secretary of State meant that the president's chief advisor on SALT would now be the administration official charged with testifying before and consulting with the Congress on U.S. strategic arms policy.

Kissinger, sensing that his new job would require considerably closer relations with Congress, attempted to call every member of the Senate Foreign Relations Committee at their respective homes the day prior to the announcement of his nomination. This was no mean feat, given the fact that the Congress was in recess at the time. However, the Secretary of State designate persisted in his efforts, having to call a number of senators several times in order to reach them. Upon reaching the various members of the committee, Kissinger pledged "a new era" in executive-legislative relations and solicited the different senators' views about how this new era might be ushered in.

On the day following his nomination to be Secretary of State, August 23, 1973, Kissinger held a news conference in San Clemente. The Secretary of State designate declared that during the first Nixon administration there was need for secrecy concerning U.S. dealings with the Soviet Union as well as China. He added, "But now we are in a different phase. The foundations that have been laid must now lead to the building of a permanent structure." To do this, Kissinger indicated that it would be necessary "to create a new consensus" and to give Congress "a stronger voice in foreign policy." When asked about whether his dual role as Presidential Assistant as well as Secretary of State would limit his testimony before Congress, Kissinger stated that one of the purposes of his nomination was "to move policy-making from the White House into the department and therefore to make it more accessible to Congress and public scrutiny." Concerning national security policy, Kissinger explicitly noted that "one of the prime objectives of the Administration will be to create a consensus in which the American people and the American Congress can understand and will support the necessity of carrying on an adequate defense program and disarmament negotiations." In regard to national security policy in particular and foreign policy in general, Kissinger pledged not to invoke the doctrine of executive privilege to withhold information from Congress except in cases in which it pertained to conversations with the president.[22]

Most senators and representatives applauded Kissinger's seemingly changed attitude toward congressional involvement in foreign and defense affairs. One senior member of both the Senate Foreign Relations and Armed Services Committees, Stuart Symington, voiced the opinion that a changed Kissinger attitude on the matter of executive-legislative relations in foreign affairs was, in fact, necessary if the Secretary of State designate wished to be confirmed. For, in Symington's words, "if there is any question about his additional work in the White House giving him executive privilege, a position he has taken in the past, I do not believe the Committee [the Senate Foreign Relations Committee] will confirm him." Frank Church summed up the views of most of his Senate colleagues when, upon learning of Kissinger's nomination, he opined: "it is time for the de facto Secretary of State to be made de jure."[23]

During the week prior to his confirmation hearings, Kissinger visited each member of the Foreign Relations Committee. In these meetings, in which Kissinger typically was not accompanied by any other administration official and senators were able to have staff present, Kissinger restated his views on the desirability of increased congressional involvement in foreign affairs. Kissinger also pledged to make himself available for consultation with members of Congress on all aspects of foreign affairs as often as such consultation seemed useful.

In a September 5 office meeting with Senator Muskie, Kissinger discussed at length the state of U.S. relations with the Soviet Union. However, when explicitly asked about the specifics of SALT II, Kissinger's responses were not forthcoming. He indicated that not much progress had been made since the second round of SALT had begun, but avoided discussion of the issues in contention and expressed the hope that the next session of SALT II, due to begin soon, would be "productive."

On the following day, Assistant Secretary of State for Congressional Relations, Marshall Wright, telephoned Senator Muskie to say that Ambassador U. Alexis Johnson would be returning to Geneva from Washington in about two weeks and that the ambassador would be happy to meet with the Maine senator to discuss SALT matters before leaving the country. Muskie agreed at once and suggested that it might be useful to have Senator Case and Paul Nitze, the Defense Department's representative on the SALT negotiating team, join the meeting. Wright concurred. On September 13, Muskie, Case, Johnson, and Nitze had lunch in Muskie's basement office at the Capitol.

Although the luncheon discussion was punctuated by roll-call votes, Johnson and Nitze briefed the two senators for more than an hour and a half on the current state of SALT, including a discussion of U.S. and Soviet strategic developments. For example, the four men talked at some length about the strategic implications of the Soviet Union's successful flight test of a MIRV the month before. Johnson and Nitze both felt that the Soviet MIRV test would make a SALT II agreement more difficult because the U.S. ability to monitor such an accord would be significantly diminished. Nitze, in particular, was worried that the Soviets seemed to be moving toward both qualitative and quantitative superiority over the United States and stressed the need for our government to prevent this from happening in any permanent SALT agreement. Nitze's concern about equality was not tied exclusively to the Soviet's MIRV capability. It was also related to the growing Soviet advantage in throw-weight, which, Nitze feared, would ultimately give the Soviet Union a superior counterforce capability. Both Johnson and Nitze urged the senators to support full funding of Trident and other strategic programs contained in the administration's Fiscal Year 1974 defense budget request which was due to come before the Senate the following week. Johnson and Nitze expressed cautious optimism about the prospects for a SALT II agreement by the end of 1974, but indicated that little substantive progress had been made thus far in Geneva.

Muskie and Case listened intently to the two members of the SALT negotiating team. Although interested in SALT, neither senator was, in fact, knowledgeable enough about the issues under debate within the U.S. government or being discussed at SALT II to challenge the assertions and figures which Johnson and Nitze employed to make their points. The simple truth was that, given the prior disinclination of the executive to discuss SALT II with Members of Congress in either private or public meetings, both senators were limited in their knowledge of the issues largely to what had appeared in the newspapers. And this often was limited to what the executive branch had decided for self-serving reasons to leak to the press.

So Muskie and Case, as the chairman and ranking member of the Foreign Relations Subcommittee charged with oversight on SALT, constituted a basically uninformed, uncritical, passive audience in their meeting with Johnson and Nitze. Nevertheless, the luncheon briefing of the two senior members of the Arms Control Subcommittee by members of the U.S. SALT negotiating team was not to be repeated during the next two years. In retrospect, one must conclude that the Johnson-Nitze luncheon with Senators Muskie and Case resulted not from a changed administration view about the importance of consulting with Members of Congress on strategic arms issues, but rather from the administration's wish to shore up congressional support for the Fiscal Year 1974 Military Procurement Authorizations Bill and to have Henry Kissinger confirmed as Secretary of State as expeditiously as possible.

In this latter regard, the administration publicly and privately urged quick Senate approval of the nomination. The point was repeatedly made that it was important that the prospective Secretary of State address the September 18 opening of the United Nations General Assembly and play an active role in the next round of SALT II, which was due to begin on September 24. It was argued that he could do both of these things most effectively if he were the Secretary of State.

The Senate was highly receptive to these entreaties, and confirmation hearings were scheduled with unusual speed. The hearings began on September 7 and lasted four days. Three days were in open session; one in executive session. Columnist William Shannon suggested that the hearings were "more pillow talk than confrontation,"[24] and in this judgment he was surely right, for the hearings were characterized for the most part by friendly interchanges between an ingratiating witness and laudatory committee members. On SALT matters, Kissinger's comments were predictably politic, general, and unrevealing. At one point, responding to the questioning of Senator Symington about the current round of SALT, Kissinger noted that "the issues in the SALT II negotiations are complex and difficult."[25] Kissinger added:

> I agree with you, Senator, about the crucial importance of SALT II.... And I agree with you that in the absence of a SALT II agreement, a permanent agreement on the limitation of strategic arms, a spiraling of the arms race is inevitable.... That agreement...should include restraints on MIRVs and other qualitative restraints, and should take account on both sides of the reality that if we don't stop the arms race now, we are going to get into a whole new realm of technology in which it will be very difficult to put the genie back into the bottle.[26]

He then remarked, "How to design qualitative restraints is a very hard question. But I can assure you of this: We are giving maximum attention to the problem."[27]

At another point in his confirmation hearings, Kissinger noted the importance of the Trident system, but suggested that he had "not studied it as fully" as some of the members of the committee.[28] At still another point, Kissinger remarked that the SALT II talks were to begin on September 24 and expressed the hope that the Senate would confirm him quickly so he could prepare for the talks.[29] All this was accepted uncritically by committee members from the chief U.S. official dealing with SALT since the start of the talks in 1969 and who, by his own admission, had "actively participated in the evolution of our position in the SALT II negotiations"[30] and who had "given more time to the problem of strategic arms limitation" than any other subject.[31]

Indeed, neither members of the Foreign Relations Committee nor other senators said anything about the prospective Secretary of State's lack of specificity, not to say candor, on SALT issues. They made little efforts to probe his views on Soviet attitudes toward the key issues under negotiation at SALT. Similarly, they did not press him to reveal in either open or closed sessions administration thinking about such key SALT II issues as MIRVs, land-mobile ICBMs, cruiser missiles, strategic bombers, anti-submarine warfare, or missile reductions. Rather, members of the Senate were content to hear that the executive branch was working on these "complex problems," and they accepted at face value Kissinger's pledges to consult regularly with the Congress on SALT matters. Never was there likely to be a better opportunity to learn of and directly affect executive thinking on SALT II matters. Yet, the opportunity was completely passed up.[32]

On September 21, the Senate approved Kissinger to be Secretary of State by a vote of 78-7. Four days later, on September 25, the SALT II negotiations resumed in Geneva. Since the talks had adjourned the previous spring two major developments had taken place: (1) the June 21, 1973 Basic Principles

Agreement, signed by President Nixon and Chairman Brezhnev, had committed the two sides to try to conclude a permanent agreement on offensive weapons by the end of 1974, and (2) on August 17, 1973, the Soviets had successfully flight-tested their first MIRV.

Needless to say, these developments put added pressure on the negotiating delegations from both sides to achieve agreement. Soon after the talks reconvened in Geneva in late September 1973, the Soviets proposed a draft SALT II treaty. The treaty, in the view of leading American officials, was "one-sided" and "outrageous."[33] They felt it sought to constrain U.S. force levels and weapons modernization without any comparable restraints on Soviet programs. The proposed draft treaty soon became known within official American circles as "the 21 Soviet demands."[34]

Besides denouncing the Soviet proposal as unacceptable, the United States delegation, in response, proposed that the Soviets consider seriously banning all future MIRV deployments and suggested that if SALT II failed, America would be forced to spend additional monies to modernize its strategic weapons. To give credence to this, Defense Secretary James Schlesinger stated at a November 30, 1973 press conference that as insurance against the failure of SALT II, he was prepared to argue for $4 billion in new strategic weapons programs in the next year's defense budget. Specifically, Schlesinger suggested that if SALT II failed to produce a permanent agreement on offensive arms, new monies would be needed for larger ICBMs, mobile land-based missiles, and an accelerated Trident submarine program.[35]

Overall, during the period from the fall of 1973-winter 1974, the key officials of the Nixon administration were not actively concerned with the matters under discussion at SALT II. Rather, they were preoccupied with developments in the Middle East, particularly the October 1973 War and the Arab oil embargo and its associated consequences. As one former National Security Council staff member has recalled, "Kissinger tends to be a one-issue man. In late 1973-early 1974, Kissinger was focused on the Middle East. He--and the administration--had little time for anything else, including SALT."[36]

As a result, although the talks in Geneva continued to go on in late 1973-early 1974, SALT policy matters were largely neglected by the executive branch and by Congress. However, with a view toward President Nixon's planned visit to Moscow in mid-1974, Secretary Kissinger undertook a trip to the Soviet Union in late March to try to achieve "a conceptual breakthrough" on SALT II. It was widely felt that if Kissinger could achieve a breakthrough with the top Soviet officials on a few key issues, the details of a new Soviet-American agreement to limit strategic arms could then be hammered out by the two delegations in a matter of six to eight weeks.

In essence, there were two major issues in dispute at

Geneva: how to limit MIRVs and what was meant by the term "equality of strategic forces." On both of these issues, there were differences not only between the American and Soviet delegations at SALT but also among American officials. Concerning the control of MIRVs, there was a significant difference of opinion between Secretary Kissinger and Secretary Schlesinger. In early 1974, Kissinger was of the opinion that the Soviet Union would not deploy missiles that they had not tested adequately and since the Soviets had only begun testing MIRVs atop their new SSX-18 missiles the previous August, they would necessarily forego further sophisticated MIRV deployments if additional MIRV testing were banned. Such a ban, Kissinger felt, would prevent improvement of the accuracy of the Soviet MIRVs, improvement which would be threatening to the United States and to global stability. Additionally, Kissinger believed that the Soviets could not be pressed too hard, too fast in the arms control area and that some agreement toward limiting MIRVs would be better than no agreement at all in terms of U.S. security and a reduction of the arms race.[37]

Within the U.S. executive branch, other officials, led by Secretary Schlesinger, did not share these views. Schlesinger felt that the United States did not have the capability to verify with certainty the number of Soviet-deployed MIRVs or, in fact, the precise nature of increasingly sophisticated Soviet MIRV deployments. Accordingly, he felt that the United States should be very tough in SALT and seek a permanent "comprehensive" agreement with the Soviets. Such an agreement would, among other things, increase the permissible number and payload of American land-based missiles and reduce the number of Soviet land-based missiles and their throw-weight. For Schlesinger such an agreement would roughly even out the nuclear strike forces on both sides; if this sort of permanent agreement could not be concluded, he argued, the United States would be better off with no SALT accord at all.[38]

Each of these approaches, of course, revolved around the meaning of what constituted equality between the two sides' strategic forces. Following ratification of the 1972 Interim Agreement by the Congress, various interpretations were placed on the requirements of the Jackson amendment to the legislation ratifying the SALT I accords. In his 1973 Foreign Policy Report to the Congress, President Nixon suggested that "any future [SALT] agreement should establish an essential equivalence in strategic capabilities among systems common to both sides."[39] At another point in the report, the president explained that "the problem of defining a balance that establishes and preserves an essential equivalency in strategic forces is no less complicated than it was four years ago. It involves the numerical levels of major systems, the capabilities of individual systems, and the overall potential of the entire strategic arsenal that each side can develop."[40]

51

In a March 4, 1974 closed-door appearance before the Senate Subcommittee on Arms Control, Secretary Schlesinger shed further light on the administration's view of "essential equivalence." Schlesinger explained: "What it means is, first, that we do not plan to have our side [be] a mirror image of their strategic forces. We do not have to have a match for everything in their arsenal. They do not have to have a match for everything in our arsenal. But in the gross characteristics of the forces, in terms of overall number and overall throw-weight or payload, there should be some degree of equivalency between the two."[41] When pressed by Senators Muskie and Humphrey on whether essential equivalence meant that the United States had to have the same numbers as the Soviets with respect to each category of nuclear weapons, Schlesinger responded: "Not for military reasons. Perhaps for political reasons in terms of perceived equality between the two forces, that may be desirable." Schlesinger added that the administration, as a whole was concentrating "in the long run on the throw-weight issue rather than on the numbers issue."[42]

Believing that Secretary Schlesinger's testimony had provided insights concerning the administration's thinking about SALT, Senator Muskie proposed in the course of Schlesinger's testimony that the subcommittee hearing be made public. Muskie explained, "If we have some of this discussion today in the public record, it could be the basis for a more sophisticated level of debate on strategic defense issues."[43] Schlesinger concurred in making the testimony public as long as it was properly "sanitized" by the executive branch. This was subsequently done, and the hearings were released to the public on April 4, 1974.

The matters of "equality" and the "numbers issues"--the question of reducing the actual numbers of Soviet and American missiles at SALT II--had, in fact, been of central concern to several senators prior to Secretary Schlesinger's appearance before the Arms Control Subcommittee in early March 1974. The previous November, Hubert Humphrey, for one, had stressed the need for our negotiators in Geneva to have a "broad approach" to the numbers issue. Specifically, in a November 30, 1973 speech, the Minnesota senator urged the United States SALT negotiating team "to begin work seriously toward actual reductions of strategic weapons" as well as "to move ahead with qualitative controls at SALT II."[44]

In a speech to the Senate on December 4, 1973, Senator Jackson also made a proposal for both SALT delegations to consider. Jackson, suggesting that the second round of strategic arms limitation talks was at an "impasse," proposed an agreement in which the Soviet Union and the United States would each be limited to 800 ICBMs (which would cut the existing Soviet ceiling in half on a strategic numerical basis); 560 SLBMs, compared with 710 launch tubes for the U.S. and 950 for the Soviets in the present, temporary five-year freeze; and

400 long-range strategic bombers, the current U.S. level being about twice the Soviet level. Jackson added that because the throw-weight of the Soviet missile force was considerably greater than that of America's force, a formula would have to be negotiated "for varying these basic numbers so as to bring the throw-weight of the two intercontinental strategic forces into approximate equality."[45]

In a speech to the Senate on February 5, 1974, Senator William Proxmire, like Jackson, urged significant reductions in U.S. and Soviet land-based forces. However, Proxmire suggested that Jackson's idea of a mutual reduction to 800 ICBMs was highly unrealistic, given the fact that the Soviet Union would have to cut their ICBM forces by 818. For Proxmire, "the crucial element in any land-based arms control after SALT I is the balancing of Soviet quantity for U.S. quality" and this called for asymmetircal, phased reductions of ICBMs. In his remarks delivered on the Senate floor, Proxmire noted:

> Undoubtedly, the U.S. has prepared a negotiating position that is sound. What, then, can a Member of Congress contribute? The following proposal...does one important thing. It says clearly that it is time to have a reduction in land-based missiles--the most threatening element of the strategic relationship. Steps must be taken to bring a systematic and orderly cutback of land-based missiles.[46]

Three days after Proxmire's speech, Senator Charles Mathias introduced legislation, Senate Resolution 283, which called on the administration to give "the highest priority" to achieving weapons reductions on a basis of "overall equality" and "overall balance" and to seek restraints on future expenditures for nuclear weapons research, development, testing, and deployment. The resolution, which was co-sponsored by thirty-five senators, stated that inequalities should be eliminated and that an agreement on the equality of the two sides' forces would "necessarily involve an overall balance in their respective forces that would take into account quantitative and qualitative differences." The resolution also stated that it was "the Sense of the Senate that the President and Secretary of State are hereby urged and requested to (a) maintain regular and full consultation with the appropriate committees of the Congress and (b) report to the Congress and the Nation at regular intervals on the progress toward further arms limitations and reductions."[47] In his Senate floor speech introducing the legislation, Mathias spoke of executive-legislative relations concerning national security policy:

> National security policy of the United States must be the result of the joint action of the Congress and the executive branch. There is no more vital national security

issue than the definition of the purpose, nature and extent of our nuclear deterrent. The United States has been engaged since 1968 in a great and profound debate on the foundations of our national security policy. This debate continues to this day. The progress and outcome of SALT I are policy reflections of this crucial national debate. It is my intention...to define in the form of a Senate resolution what [I] think the future course of U.S. policy in strategic weapons should be. This resolution is focused upon the SALT II talks. We introduce this resolution at this time, because we believe that the Congress and the Administration should work together closely so that we can arrive at a jointly approved national security policy for the SALT talks at Geneva and to lay down guidelines for our future strategic policy that the Congress and the country can fully support.[48]

The proposal which Kissinger ultimately put forward in Moscow in late March 1974 was an amalgamation of his own views, those of Secretary Schlesinger, and some of those expressed in the Senate. Kissinger's proposal, which marked a departure from past administration policy, called for conditional halting of further MIRV deployments as part of a new, overall agreement on offensive nuclear weapons. The condition which Kissinger sought to impose was that the Soviets would agree to limit their future deployment of those types of MIRV systems in which the United States exercised a substantial lead over the Soviets. In addition to offering to stop the deployment of MIRVs on a conditional basis, the American proposal put forward in Moscow called for (1) equalizing the total throw-weight of both sides' MIRVs; (2) no limitations on the payloads of long-range bombers or missiles without MIRVs; and (3) equalizing the total numbers of missiles and strategic bombers on both sides.[49]

Somewhat predictably, the Soviets were negatively disposed toward the American MIRV proposals, given the substantial U.S. lead in deployments in this area. In addition, the Soviets felt that such systems as American tactical aircraft stationed in Europe and British nuclear submarines should be included in any comprehensive agreement. So, while Kissinger's trip to Moscow did give the American Secretary of State and the top Russian leaders a chance to interchange ideas on the major problems stalling SALT II, it did not produce the "breakthrough" for which Kissinger had hoped.[50]

Upon his return to the United States from Moscow via several Western European capitals, Kissinger briefed the Senate Foreign Relations Committee on his trip. He talked about the current state of Middle East negotiations. He explained European concerns about U.S.-European economic relations. And he discussed his conversations about SALT with the Soviet leadership. In this last regard, Kissinger made it clear that no comprehensive SALT agreement would be concluded during President Nixon's approaching visit to Moscow. The Secretary of State did, however, express hope that an interim SALT accord would result from the trip and explained that some progress had, in fact, been made in his talks in Moscow. Kissinger stressed, though, that significant differences about the nature of a SALT II agreement still existed between the two sides. Specifically, he noted that the Soviets were unlikely to agree to any American proposal which gave the United States an advantage in the number of land-based missiles with multiple warheads. In addition, Kissinger suggested that the Soviets were not amenable to the idea of equalizing the total number of missiles and bombers on each side, unless the United States agreed to include its forward-based systems stationed in Europe.

In their questioning, the members of the committee tried to get the Secretary of State to elaborate on the details of these points. They also tried to explore possible differences of opinion between Kissinger and Secretary Schlesinger on SALT matters. For example, at one point in the hearing, Senator Muskie noted that Secretary Schlesinger had told the Arms Control Subcommittee at a March 4 meeting that the United States ought to seek to have "a limitation on numbers that is fully applicable to both sides and a limitation on throw-weight that would be hypothetically applicable to both sides." Muskie then asked Kissinger if this viewpoint would be acceptable to the Secretary of State, to the Nixon administration, and to the Soviet leaders. Kissinger, in reply, tartly declared that in Moscow and before the committee he was speaking for the administration, not just for a given member of it, and that the press had tried to create a non-existent rift between Schlesinger and himself on SALT issues. On the Schlesinger proposal concerning limiting numbers and throw-weight, Kissinger suggested that this was a worthy objective for the U.S. SALT negotiating team to pursue but noted that it was unlikely the Soviets would agree to such a formulation. When pressed by several committee members--notably Muskie, Humphrey, and Case-- for the details of an agreement the Soviets were likely to accept, Kissinger noted that in his talks in Moscow, the Soviets continued to insist that an acceptable agreement would have to provide for both a Soviet throw-weight advantage and equal numbers of land-based MIRVs. When asked whether such an agreement would be in America's interest as part of a total package, the Secretary of State replied that he preferred to respond to that and associated matters in a separate hearing, perhaps before the Arms Control Subcommittee, and that he would welcome the opportunity to discuss U.S. SALT policy in detail with committee members.

This was not the first time that Kissinger had suggested that he would welcome a specific Foreign Relations Committee or Subcommittee hearing on SALT II. He had made this suggestion in response to committee members' questions about U.S. SALT policies at several prior hearings, including his confirmation hearings to be Secretary of State. The fact was, however, that no such hearing had ever taken place. On every occasion that members of the Foreign Relations Committee or their staffs had tried to arrange such a meeting with the Secretary of State, they had been told by Kissinger's aides that a hearing on SALT II, although welcomed by the Secretary, was impossible to schedule at that time. The simple fact is, to underscore a key point, at no time in the years 1973-76 did Secretary Kissinger meet with the Foreign Relations Committee or its Arms Control Subcommittee to discuss in detail U.S. SALT policy.

Near the end of his March post-Moscow briefing, Kissinger told the Foreign Relations Committee members that the shadow of the Watergate scandal, which was growing increasingly large in the course of the winter and spring of 1974, had negatively affected his trip to Russia. Kissinger expressed the fear that Soviet leaders were becoming reluctant to enter into a new SALT agreement with the Nixon administration because they were concerned about whether or not the executive branch could get congressional backing for any new treaty. Kissinger then urged committee members to resolve the pending Watergate debate as quickly as possible so that the SALT negotiations could go forward, unimpeded by domestic political concerns.

Senator Henry Jackson, for one, did little to allay the Soviets' fears or Kissinger's concerns. On the contrary, in a highly-publicized speech to the Overseas Press Club on April 22, 1974, Jackson sharply attacked the Nixon administration's approach to SALT II in both national security and domestic political terms, implying at one point that the administration was employing a "quick fix" approach to SALT for domestic political purposes.

In the speech, Jackson restated his December 4, 1973 proposal for missile reductions and explained his disenchantment with the executive branch's approach to SALT in the following manner:

> ...rather than concentrating on the design and presentation of an arms control proposal that could form the basis for a long-term stabilization of the strategic balance, the Administration has concentrated on quick-fix, short term proposals that can be readied in time for the forthcoming June summit meeting in Moscow.... There is nothing unique about the month of June that would justify an extension of the SALT I interim agreement and thereby legitimize its terms beyond 1977 and prejudice the prospects for a meaningful and stabilizing SALT II treaty. I am not content to let the matter rest upon the complex and multi-purpose judgments of an embattled White House....[51]

When President Nixon finally went to Moscow in late June-early July 1974, he did not carry with him an agreed-upon, government-wide position.[52] Not surprisingly, the trip did not, in fact, produce a permanent agreement to limit strategic offensive arms. However, the trip was not without arms control significance. In the administration's words, "the two leaders [Nixon and Brezhnev] held the most extensive discussions of the arms race that have ever taken place, with a frankness that would have been considered inconceivable two years ago."[53]

In addition, some five arms agreements were concluded during the 1974 summit. First, the two countries jointly agreed to seek a ten-year accord on offensive arms; this was seen as a more realistic goal than the "permanent" agreement initially envisioned. Second, a protocol to the 1972 ABM treaty was signed which eliminated the option under the earlier agreement to build a second ABM site.[54] Third, a threshold test ban agreement was concluded. This accord prohibited underground nuclear weapons testing above the threshold of 150 kilotons of explosive power. Due to enter into force on March 31, 1976, this Treaty on the Limitation of Underground Nuclear Weapons, as initially drawn up, did not affect peaceful nuclear explosions.[55] Finally, Secretary Kissinger and Foreign Minister Gromyko signed two agreements resulting from the work of the Standing Consultative Commission (SCC), the permanent joint U.S.-Soviet body set up following SALT I to supervise the agreements. The first of the documents signed in Moscow set forth "general guidelines and specific procedures for dismantling or destroying older land-based ICBM launchers and older submarine ballistic missile launchers when they are replaced." The second agreement established guidelines for "dismantling or destroying ABM launchers which are in excess of treaty limits."[56]

It was not accidental that two agreements resulting from the work of the Standing Consultative Commission were signed during President Nixon's trip to the Soviet Union. In the week prior to the president's departure for Moscow, Paul Nitze, formerly the Chief Defense Department representative on the U.S. SALT delegation, testified before the Senate Armed Services Subcommittee on SALT, chaired by Henry Jackson. Nitze had resigned his government position the previous week because of the burgeoning effect the Watergate scandal was having on SALT and also because of Secretary Kissinger's penchant for not using the negotiating team in Geneva for key SALT discussions with the Soviets. In closed-door testimony before Jackson's subcommittee on June 20, 1974, Nitze explained that the administration had left certain loopholes in the SALT I Interim Agreement and then—unbeknownst to most of the executive branch and to the entire Congress—secretly attempted to eliminate the ambiguities in the accord. Nitze noted that Secretary Kissinger had met with Soviet Ambassador Dobrynin on July 24, 1972, two months after the May 1972 summit in Moscow, and signed an "interpretation" of the accords. The "interpretation" was designed to clarify whether any Soviet modernization of their older diesel submarines would be counted against the publicly announced 950 ceiling placed on them by the Interim Agreement.[57] According to one account, still further "clarification" on this point was needed, and it was only after an agreement was signed by Kissinger and Dobrynin in Washington on June 17, 1974, concerning Soviet replacement of old diesel submarines, that this loophole in the Interim Agreement had been closed.[58]

On the day following Nitze's secret testimony, two members of the SALT subcommittee, Senators Symington and Jackson, publicly criticized the administration's handling of the SALT I accords. In an intentionally understated comment, Symington declared that he had found Nitze's testimony disquieting and suggested that in regard to the Interim Agreement's ceiling on submarines, "the figures we got aren't the right figures."[59]

Jackson was far more outspoken in his attack on the administration, attempting, in the words of one observer "[to cast] a pall over Kissinger's credibility on the eve of the SALT summit."[60] In a press conference called to discuss the so-called "Kissinger-Dobrynin loophole," Jackson denounced in no uncertain terms Kissinger's attempts to conceal and subsequently clandestinely eliminate ambiguities contained in the Interim Agreement. While indicating that the "Kissinger-Dobrynin loophole" would not likely "upset the balance of power" between American and Soviet forces, Jackson noted that it did constitute "a substantial alteration of the agreement as represented to the Congress" and implied that the Nixon administration, by not submitting the secret understandings to Congress, was in violation of the Arms Control and Disarmament Act of 1961. Jackson then made the additional charge that President Nixon and Secretary Kissinger had given the Russians a pledge during the 1972 summit that the United States would not build the maximum allowable American submarine missile launchers permitted by the Interim Agreement.[61]

In subsequent testimony before both Jackson's SALT subcommittee and the Foreign Relations Committee, Kissinger vigorously denied Jackson's charges, labelling them "totally false." Kissinger admitted that the text of the American-Soviet "interpretation" agreed to following the 1972 summit meeting had not been reported in written form to Congress, for "it was in the channel of communications between President Nixon and Secretary Brezhnev." However, Kissinger insisted that the "substance" of the "interpretation" had been communicated to Congress and that the missile totals under the Interim Agreement had not been "changed by any agreement, understanding, or clarification--public or private."[62]

As for Jackson's second charge--that the Nixon administration had given a secret pledge to Secretary Brezhnev to limit itself to only 656 submarine missiles instead of the 710 authorized--Kissinger said that on the final day of the 1972 summit meeting, President Nixon "put into the agreement a right which we had no intention to exercise," to deploy up to the maximum number of submarine-launched nuclear missiles by 1977. Kissinger indicated that for the president to tell this to the Soviets "was not a concession" but only "a relatively minor gesture designed to regain general confidence."[63] When asked why this "prediction" on American submarine building plans was not submitted to Congress, Kissinger replied that the fact was generally known.[64]

While much debate, a good deal of controversy, and some ill will were engendered by this discussion of alleged ambiguities and secret pledges concerning the SALT I accords, three points are clear. First, in the course of the June-July 1974 summit in Moscow following Paul Nitze's testimony before Congress, new agreements were concluded between the United States and the Soviet Union specifying procedures for the dismantling or destruction of older submarine ballistic missile launchers or older land-based ICBM launchers that were to be replaced and for the dismantling of ABM launchers that were in excess of treaty limits. Second, the revelations about loopholes in the Interim Agreement and the executive branch's covert efforts to close these loopholes raised some serious questions in the minds of many senators and representatives concerning the administration's commitment to keep Congress fully informed about SALT, particularly regarding possible Soviet violations of the 1972 accords. Third, the interchange between Kissinger and the Armed Services Subcommittee on SALT constituted a significant effort on the part of Congress to hold the executive branch accountable for its stewardship in the area of U.S. SALT policy.

At a July 3, 1974 press conference following the summit meeting in Moscow, Secretary Kissinger answered a question on nuclear forces with a question of his own--"What in God's name is strategic superiority?" Subsequently, the Secretary of State declared that the American people should have a chance to debate this and related questions about détente and national security, and he expressed his eagerness to participate in such a debate after he returned to Washington.[65] In truth, Kissinger's call for a debate on U.S.-Soviet relations never really took place. Soon after President Nixon and Kissinger returned from Moscow, impeachment proceedings were underway. By early August 1974, Richard Nixon had resigned from the presidency, and the first weeks of the administration of Gerald Ford were occupied by many concerns other than those regarding SALT II. Accordingly, when Secretary Kissinger testified on "détente" before the Foreign Relations Committee on September 20, 1974, he was forced to admit that no "concrete proposal" on specific numbers of nuclear weapons to be limited by SALT II accords had been agreed upon inside the Ford administration. He did suggest, though, that he was optimistic such a proposal would be agreed to prior to his planned trip to Moscow in October. Responding to questions from several committee members about why there was no unified administration policy on SALT, Kissinger repeatedly denied that there were any major differences between Secretary Schlesinger and himself. At one point in the questioning, Kissinger insisted: "There is no struggle going on. There are occasional differences of emphasis. There is no power struggle."[66] When questioned about various possible U.S. positions at SALT, the secretary once again suggested that he would welcome a special hearing with the committee to discuss SALT matters specifically. But once again, when efforts were subsequently made by staff aides to Foreign Relations Committee members to arrange such a hearing, Kissinger's assistants at the State Department explained that the secretary's schedule would not permit it at that time.

The SALT II talks officially resumed on September 18, 1974, after a recess of several months. While talks were going on in Geneva in late September-early October of 1974--the American delegation was without negotiating instructions from the Ford administration--several National Security Council meetings were held in Washington to hammer out a new U.S. SALT negotiating position. President Ford presided at the NSC meetings, which were characterized by frequently heated debates between Secretaries Kissinger and Schlesinger on possible U.S. negotiating stances.

The issues and respective arguments of the two men were much the same as they had been during the previous twelve months. In essence, Secretary Schlesinger argued that "we must face the Soviets down" on their desire to deploy a large number of missiles with multiple warheads or, failing that, "buckle down for a five-year, all-out arms race."[67] Schlesinger told the president that if Ford wished to postpone reductions in forces and controls on modernization, he had a choice of insisting either on overall equality of strategic forces or on such a low MIRV ceiling that neither side would be inclined to take advantage of the other.[68]

Secretary Kissinger argued that the Soviets would never accept the terms that Schlesinger wanted to insist on and that if a new agreement was not reached soon, a new arms race in MIRVs would likely begin, which might jeopardize the 1972 ABM Treaty. In support of his arguments, Kissinger cited CIA studies showing that the Soviets were planning to deploy at least 3,000 delivery vehicles and 1,500-2,000 MIRVs over the next five years. Kissinger argued that an all-out arms race was not politically feasible--a judgment the Joint Chiefs of Staff shared--and that the United States should pursue a step-by-step approach of high ceilings for the present time, followed by reductions and controls on modernization later on.

With the Joint Chiefs of Staff favoring Kissinger's proposals, which would allow them to complete their MIRV modernization programs, and with President Ford playing a passive role, the last of a series of three mid-October NSC meetings produced a U.S. proposal, the terms of which were: (1) an equal delivery vehicle ceiling of about 2,000; (2) an equal number (approximately 1,000) of missiles with multiple warheads; and (3) sub-limits on large Soviet land-based missiles (e.g., SS-9s or SS-18s) and American bomber-launched missiles. If the Soviets rejected this, the plan was for the United States to revert to the old proposal of a Soviet lead in delivery vehicles and an American advantage in numbers of MIRVs.[69]

Soon thereafter, on October 20, Kissinger left for Moscow. The new proposal which the secretary carried with him was known only to a very small part of the SALT bureaucracy and was completely unknown to Members of Congress.

The Soviet leadership's initial reaction to the proposal was surprisingly favorable, although Brezhnev and Foreign Minister Gromyko wanted time to scrutinize it further. Some four weeks later, President Ford and Secretary Brezhnev met in Vladivostok to get acquainted and to discuss the new American proposal. To the surprise of many, on the second day of talks the two leaders agreed that further SALT II negotiations would be based on the following principles: (1) an overall delivery vehicle ceiling for both sides of 2,400; (2) a ceiling of 1,320 on MIRVs; (3) if a missile had been tested with multiple warheads, every missile of that kind would be counted against the 1,320 MIRV ceiling; (4) land-mobile missiles and bomber-launched strategic missiles could be deployed, but were to be included within the overall ceiling; (5) a limit of 300 on the big Soviet land-based missiles (e.g., SS-9s, SS-18s) when deployed, with no new silos to be built; (6) a new agreement would include provision for further negotiations beginning no later than 1980-81 on the question of further limitations and possible reductions of strategic arms after 1985; and (7) negotiations between the American and Soviet delegations to work out the new agreement incorporating the foregoing points would resume in Geneva in January 1975.[70]

Unlike the SALT I agreement, the Vladivostok Accord provided for an exact equivalence between the United States and the Soviet Union in numbers of strategic weapons. Senator Jackson's principle of equality had been embodied in the agreement. Balance between the two sides was not provided for, however, in regard to such matters as numbers of warheads or throw-weight, issues not covered by the agreement. Nor were the Soviets' Backfire bombers or the Americans' cruise missiles covered by the accord.

While President Ford and Secretary Kissinger hailed the agreement as a significant step in "capping" the arms race, reaction to the Vladivostok Accord on Capitol Hill was mixed. Senator Jackson, after a White House briefing, assailed the MIRV figure as "astonishingly large" and urged his congressional colleagues "to let the administration know that it must go back and negotiate a treaty that provides for substantial, mutual, long-range phased reductions."[71] Senator Goldwater challenged Kissinger's claim that the agreement "caps the arms race" and suggested that it was "just another ploy by the Russians to try to fool some of our détente-happy people."[72] Senators Kennedy, Mathias, and Mondale introduced a Sense of the Senate Resolution in support of "the broad purposes of the agreement" but calling on the president to use the Vladivostok Accord as a starting point to "make every possible effort to negotiate further nuclear arms limitation and reduction." In their resolution, which was introduced on December 13, 1974, one week before the 93rd Congress adjourned, the three senators specifically urged the president to seek agreements on lower number levels, both for overall missile strength and for MIRVs; restraints on the pace of deployment of weapons systems within these lower levels; and limits on the annual number of missile flight tests.[73] Other senators wondered how compliance with the agreement would be verified, while still other Members of Congress criticized Part V of the aide-memoire which stated that further negotiations should begin no later than 1980 on arms reductions to occur after 1985. These senators argued that such a provision seemed to preclude the possibility of earlier reductions.[74]

Hoping to increase support for the Vladivostok Accord in the Congress, Kissinger undertook negotiations with the Soviets in mid-December to modify Section V of the Vladivostok aide-memoire. In this, Kissinger was soon successful, and in a December 30, 1974 interview with <u>Newsweek</u>, the Secretary of State declared publicly that:

> The Vladivostok announcement...said that negotiations should start no later than 1980 for reductions to take place after 1985. That has now been eliminated from the aide-memoire...negotiations can start as soon as possible and take effect as soon as there is an agreement.[75]

In early January 1975, before the 94th Congress convened, members of the staffs of Senators Kennedy, Mathias, and Mondale met on several occasions with Kissinger aides William Hyland and Helmut Sonnenfeldt to discuss the Vladivostok Accord. The congressional and executive staffers also discussed at length the December 13, 1974 Senate resolution concerning the Vladivostok Accord. All of these staffers agreed that it would be useful to line up substantial congressional backing for the sense of the Senate resolution in support of the Vladivostok agreements, in part to "give the White House some 'backbone' against its critics on the right."[76] However, Hyland and Sonnenfeldt, at Kissinger's direction, argued that certain changes would have to be made in the resolution before the administration could support it. Among other things, they argued for the elimination of the part of the resolution which called on the administration to make "every possible effort" to limit the number of missile flight tests each year. Acting at the direction of their principals, the congressional staffers soon agreed to this and other minor changes in the resolution, provided that the administration would: (1) publicly support the legislation when it was reintroduced in modified form in the next Congress, (2) actively help line up additional co-sponsors of the legislation, and (3) follow the directives contained in the resolution. On these points, the administration representatives agreed.[77]

Consequently, on January 17, 1975, Senators Kennedy, Mathias, and Mondale introduced Senate Resolution 20. The key part of the legislation declared it the advice of the Senate that the president should make "every possible effort" (1) to complete the negotiations resulting from the Vladivostok agreement and (2) to reach further agreements on matters including: (a) lower numbers, both for overall missile strength and for MIRVs; (b) restraints on pace and character of developments and deployments of strategic weapons within these lower numbers; and (c) further mutual limitations with regard to arms not limited as part of the 1972 strategic arms control accords and the Vladivostok agreement.[78]

The legislation, termed "advice" from the Senate, represented a Senate first. Under Article II, Section 2 of the Constitution, the Senate is to give its advice and consent on treaties, i.e., binding commitments on the part of the United States with foreign nations. As explained by Senator Mathias, Senate Resolution 20 was neither a law nor a Sense-of-the-Senate resolution, "but a way to add gravity to senatorial views on foreign affairs." Mathias went on to explain:

> In accord with the Constitution, the Senate should give its advice on what the policy of the United States should be; the executive branch should carry out this advice in the form of negotiations, and the result of these negotiations, that is, treaties, should undergo a process of ratification, that is, consent. Despite the power given to the Senate by the Constitution, it is remarkable that there have been no recorded instances of the use of formal "advice" in the history of our Government.[79]

On the afternoon that the resolution was introduced in the Senate, Secretary Kissinger, in accordance with the agreement previously worked out at the staff level, publicly announced that the administration "welcomed" the legislation.[80] However, Kissinger and other key administration officials then proceeded to renege on the rest of the agreement: they declined to rally Senate support behind the legislation or to follow in any perceptible way the "advice" contained therein. Specifically, once the legislation had been introduced on January 17 and the senators most interested in arms control had agreed to co-sponsor it, the administration seemingly opted to disregard the legislation and refused to help secure its passage. Indeed, the administration appeared to prefer that the Senate as a whole not be on record in support of advice to the executive branch on SALT. In part as a result of the administration's negativism toward Senate Resolution 20 and in part as a result of the general lack of congressional interest in SALT matters, the legislation lay moribund within the Senate Foreign Relations Committee for the entire 94th Congress and never came to a vote on the Senate floor.[81]

Faced with no legislative action on Senate Resolution 20 and little visible progress at the SALT II talks in Geneva, Senators Alan Cranston, Bill Brock, Charles Mathias, and six of the nine members of the Foreign Relations Subcommittee on Arms Control introduced Senate Concurrent Resolution 69 on October 9, 1975. Cranston, in introducing the legislation, declared that the resolution "represented an effort to induce a laggard Congress and hesitant White House to focus in on this issue [SALT II] and, hopefully, to come up with--at long, long last--a compelling act of statesmanship that will halt the world's silent slide into nuclear proliferation and disaster."[82] The resolution, which addressed several aspects of the proliferation issue, called for ratification of the Vladivostok Accords. This was to be followed "immediately" by negotiations for a verifiable, mutual twenty per cent cut in nuclear weapons in order to reduce the high ceiling for strategic missiles and bombers by the Vladivostok Accord.[83]

Some four months later, on February 25, 1976, a group of senators, led by Edward Kennedy, introduced Senate Resolution 399 which was explicitly aimed at putting the Senate on record regarding SALT II. Like Kennedy's January 1975 resolution and Cranston's October 1975 resolution, this bill expressed support for the conclusion of negotiations to implement the Vladivostok agreement. However, to the chagrin of the White House, it also went further than any previous resolution in proposing specific limits on air-launched cruise missiles. It suggested that the president should seek agreement with Soviet leaders "to ban flight testing and deployment by either country of air-launched cruise missiles having a range in excess of 2500 kilometers." It also called for "a ban of the flight testing or deployment by either country of land-launched and sea-launched cruise missiles having ranges in excess of 600 kilometers." Finally, it proposed that the president offer the Soviets an immediate, mutual moratorium on the flight testing of all strategic-range cruise missiles. The moratorium would remain in effect until the conclusion of the rest of the agreement called for in the legislation.[84]

This resolution, which was introduced without prior consultation with any executive branch officials, reflected dissatisfaction on the part of its sponsors with what had happened after the introduction of Senate Resolution 20, the virtual non-involvement of the Senate in the ongoing process by which U.S. SALT policy was made, and the general lack of progress at SALT II. The fact is that in the period from the conclusion of the Vladivostok Accord in November 1974 through the end of 1976, despite hopeful executive branch pronouncements to the contrary, there was little concrete progress at SALT.[85]

In essence, in the 1974-76 years, a SALT II treaty was hung up over three issues: (1) limitations on cruise missiles; (2) limitations on strategic bombers, and (3) verification of limitations on MIRVs. At different times during the last two years of the Ford administration, both sides offered various proposals to resolve these issues.[86] But at no time were the two sides able to agree on the details of a new SALT accord, and an agreement became increasingly less likely as the 1976 American elections approached and U.S. domestic politics--particularly Ronald Reagan's challenge to Gerald Ford--impinged on U.S. SALT policy considerations. Hence, during the more than two years from the conclusion of the Vladivostok Accord in November 1974 until the end of 1976, SALT II continued to go on in Geneva, but with little concrete accomplishment.

A SUMMING UP

As in SALT I, the Senate generally did not play a very meaningful role in the formulation of U.S. SALT policy during the 1972-76 period. In the roughly four years between the beginning of the second round of SALT in November 1972 and the end of 1976, the executive branch exercised a dominant influence in the policy process, while the Senate was by and large content to support and acquiesce in executive branch policy.

To say this, though, is not to deny the interest and to some extent indirect influence of several individual senators--notably Case, Cranston, Humphrey, Jackson, Kennedy, Mathias, Mondale, and Muskie--on the SALT II negotiations. Jackson, in particular, set the general framework within which all of the SALT II discussions took place with his amendment to the 1972 Interim Agreement which called for equality between the forces of the United States and the Soviet Union. Jackson also helped to hold the executive branch accountable for its stewardship of the SALT negotiations through SALT subcommittee hearings he chaired on possible loopholes in and violations of the SALT I accords. Muskie, to cite another example, through hearings of the Arms Control Subcommittee, sporadically pressed administration officials in 1973-74 to defend U.S. strategic policy and in so doing helped broaden the terms of the debate on SALT policy.

On the whole, though, Senate involvement in the policy

process by which the U.S. negotiating posture at SALT II was formulated and implemented was extremely limited. The overwhelming majority of senators as well as the responsible committees and subcommittees did not keep themselves closely informed about the issues under negotiation or U.S. positions on those issues. They did not develop policy alternatives on their own or, by and large, challenge executive positions. To the extent they were involved, they participated passively in pro forma executive-initiated briefings on SALT and occasionally considered non-binding legislative resolutions. During the 1972-76 years, not only did the Senate not enact any legislation binding the executive branch regarding SALT, but it did not even enact any advisory Sense-of-the-Senate resolutions. In short, the executive branch dominated the SALT II policy process in much the same way it had dominated SALT I.

NOTES

1. Richard Nixon, "U.S. Policy for the 1970's: A Report to the Congress." May 31, 1973, p. 202.
2. NYT, March 13, 1973.
3. It should be noted that this stricture which was respected by most senators and representatives, had the ancillary effect of lessening the number of probing questions that Members of Congress and their staffs posed to Johnson about SALT issues.
4. Letter from Philip Farley to Senator Edmund S. Muskie, February 24, 1973.
5. Letter from Senator Edmund Muskie and Senator Clifford Case to U. Alexis Johnson, March 9, 1973.
6. Letter from U. Alexis Johnson to Senator Edmund Muskie, March 27, 1973.
7. NYT, March 20, 1973.
8. "SALT II: Can the Arms Race Be Ended?" (Washington: Government Printing Office, 1974), p. 8.
9. Ibid., p. 10.
10. Foreign Affairs (January 1973): 282.
11. Statement of Senator Edmund S. Muskie on the Nomination of Fred Iklé to be Director of the Arms Control and Disarmament Agency, Press Release, April 6, 1973.
12. Letter from J. William Fulbright to Hubert Humphrey, May 20, 1973.
13. Letter from Hubert Humphrey to J. William Fulbright, May 24, 1973. See Dine, pp. 47-48.
14. See WP, June 14, 1973.
15. The confirmation hearings of Amron Katz and Robert Behr followed Iklé's hearing. Their hearings were, if anything, less informative regarding SALT matters than Iklé's appearance before the committee. Nevertheless, all three men were confirmed overwhelmingly by the committee and the full Senate.

16. "Briefing on Major Foreign Policy Questions," Hearings before the Foreign Relations Committee with Secretary of State William Rogers, February 21, 1973. U.S. Senate, 93rd Congress, 1st Session, 1973, p. 12.

17. See "Nomination of Elliot Richardson to be Sectetary of Defense and William Clements to be Deputy Secretary of Defense," Hearing before the Committee on Armed Services, U.S. Senate, 93rd Congress, January 9-12, 1973, pp. 68-70, 91-92, 164-65.

18. See "Nomination of James R. Schlesinger to be Secretary of Defense," Hearing before the Committee on Armed Services, June 18, 1973, U.S. Senate, 93rd Congress, 1st Session, pp. 61-62.

19. Interview with William Rogers by Vladimir Vashedschenko, Washington bureau chief of TASS, Press Release of the Department of State, June 14, 1973.

20. NYT, May 13, 1973.

21. See WP, June 22, 1973. For a full statement of the agreed-on principles, see "Basic Principles of Negotiations on the Further Limitation of Strategic Offensive Arms, signed at Washington, June 21, 1973," which is reprinted in NYT, June 22, 1973.

22. NYT, August 24, 1973.

23. Ibid.

24. Ibid., September 13, 1973.

25. "Hearings before the Foreign Relations Committee on the Nomination of Henry Kissinger to be Secretary of State, September 7, 10, 11, and 14, 1973." U.S. Senate, 93rd Congress, 1st Session, p. 121.

26. Ibid.

27. Ibid.

28. Ibid., p. 300.

29. Ibid., p. 44.

30. Ibid., p. 45.

31. Ibid., p. 121.

32. Interestingly, while content to accept Kissinger's pro forma responses to questions about SALT II, the Foreign Relations Committee was not willing to accept his answers to their inquiries about his role in the 1969-71 wiretapping of certain administration officials and newspapermen. At one point, committee members hinted that if Kissinger was not more forthcoming about his role in the wiretapping, his confirmation as Secretary of State might be in jeopardy. Soon thereafter, Kissinger arranged to have theretofore secret Justice Department documents on wiretapping made available to two senior members of the committee. See "Nomination of Henry Kissinger," pp. 11-15, 266-99.

33. NYT, December 5, 1973.

34. Ibid.

35. Ibid., December 1, 1973.

36. Interview with Philip Odeen, June 25, 1976.

37. Confidential Interview. See also NYT, February 6, 1974 and WP, June 15, 1974.
38. Confidential Interview. Also, see Luther Carter, "Strategic Arms Limitation (II): 'Leveling up' to Symmetry," Science 187 (February 21, 1975): 13-17.
39. Richard Nixon, "U.S. Foreign Policy for the 1970's," A Report to the Congress, May 3, 1973, p. 204.
40. Ibid.
41. "Hearing on U.S.-U.S.S.R. Strategic Policies" before the Subcommittee on Arms Control, International Law and Organization, Committee on Foreign Relations, 93rd Congress, 2d Session, March 4, 1974 (Washington: Government Printing Office, 1974), p. 41.
42. Ibid., p. 42.
43. Ibid.
44. See "Nuclear Arms Limitations: Congress is Wary," Congressional Quarterly, June 15, 1974, pp. 1546-1547.
45. Senator Henry Jackson, "SALT: An Analysis and a Proposal," Congressional Record, December 4, 1973, pp. S21757-9. Also, see WP, December 5, 1973.
46. Senator William Proxmire, "A SALT II Proposal," Congressional Record, February 5, 1974, p. S1195.
47. Congressional Record, February 8, 1974, p. S1597.
48. Ibid.
49. NYT, March 31, 1974. Confidential Interview.
50. Confidential Interview. See NYT, March 31, 1974.
51. "Detente and SALT," reprinted in the Congressional Record, April 23, 1974, p. S6065-7. During the winter of 1974, the House Armed Services Committee set up a Special Subcommittee on Arms Control and Disarmament to hold hearings on SALT and the members of the subcommittee--Chairman Charles Wilson, John Murtha, and Floyd Spence--all expressed reservations about the administration's approach to SALT II similar to those of Senator Jackson. Review of Arms Control and Disarmament Activities, U.S. House of Representatives, 93rd Congress, 2d Session (Washington: Government Printing Office, 1974). The special subcommittee was not reconstituted in the 94th Congress.
52. Confidential Interview. Also see Jacquelyn Davis, et al., SALT II and the Search for Strategic Equivalence (Philadelphia: Foreign Policy Research Institute, 1975), p. 61.
53. "Arms Limitation Agreements--July 1974 Summit," U.S. Arms Control and Disarmament Agency, Publication 73 (July 1974), p. 1.
54. The ABM protocol was submitted to the Senate in September 1974 and ratified without much debate in 1975. The 1974 ABM protocol left the Soviets with an ABM system around Moscow and the United States with an ABM system around U.S. Minuteman base in Grand Forks, North Dakota. As of July 1, 1976, the U.S. ABM system in Grand Forks was closed down.

55. On May 28, 1976, a companion treaty to the threshold test treaty was concluded to govern peaceful nuclear explosions. The companion agreement, known as the Treaty on Underground Nuclear Explosions for Peaceful Purposes, and the Treaty on the Limitation of Underground Nuclear Weapons are currently being considered for ratification by the Senate. For more discussion of congressional interest in the threshold test ban agreement, see "Congress and Foreign Policy: 1974," A Report Prepared for the House Committee on International Relations by the Congressional Research Service of the Library of Congress, April 15, 1975 (Washington: Government Printing Office, 1975), pp. 21-22.

56. "Arms Limitation Agreements--July 1974 Summit," p. 4.

57. Confidential Interview. For further discussion of Nitze's testimony before the SALT subcommittee, see Leslie Gelb, "The Story of a Flap," Foreign Policy 16 (Fall 1974): 168-70. Also, WP, June 22, 1974.

58. NYT, June 22, 1974. For a detailed discussion of this issue, see Elmo Zumwalt, On Watch: A Memoir (New York: Quadrangle, 1976).

59. Gelb, p. 168.

60. Ibid., p. 181.

61. NYT, June 22, 1974.

62. WP, June 25, 1974.

63. Ibid, June 25, 1972.

64. Ibid.

65. NYT, July 4, 1974. Also, see NYT, July 30, 1974.

66. WP, September 19, 1974.

67. NYT, December 3, 1974.

68. Ibid. Also, Carter, pp. 12-14.

69. NYT, December 3, 1974. Also, see Aviation Week and Space Technology, December 9, 1974, p. 7.

70. NYT, November 25, 1974 and December 3, 1974. "Arms Control and Disarmament Agreements: Tests and History of Negotiations," U.S. Arms Control and Disarmament Agency, February 1975, pp. 129-30.

71. NYT, December 5, 1974 and December 8, 1974.

72. WP, December 3, 1974.

73. Congressional Record, December 13, 1974.

74. See "Congress and Foreign Policy: 1974," p. 22.

75. Newsweek, December 30, 1974, p. 29.

76. Congressional Quarterly, November 29, 1975, p. 2584. Confidential Interview.

77. Interview with Robert Hunter, July 29, 1976.

78. Congressional Record, January 19, 1975, p. S463. Among the weapons limitations not covered by previous agreements were limits on cruise missiles, mobile missiles, and a comprehensive test ban.

79. Congressional Record, January 17, 1975, p. S463.

80. See NYT, January 18, 1975.

81. Interview with Robert Hunter, July 29, 1976. Inter-

view with William Miller, July 30, 1976. Legislation similar to Senate Resolution 20 was introduced in the House of Representatives in early 1975 by Representatives Zablocki, Bingham, et al., but it also foundered in committee. The House International Relations Committee did, however, hold a series of penetrating hearings in 1975 on the Vladivostok Accord. See "The Vladivostok Accord: Implications to United States Security and Arms Control and World Peace," Committee on International Relations, U.S. House of Representatives, 94th Congress, 1st Session (Washington: Government Printing Office, 1975).

    82. Congressional Record, October 9, 1975, p. S18099.
    83. Ibid.
    84. Ibid., February 25, 1976, p. S2289.
    85. Confidential Interview.
    86. For discussion of the details of these proposals, see William Beecher's three-part series on SALT II in The Boston Globe, July 7-9, 1976. Also, see Luther Carter, "Beyond Vladivostok," Science 188 (April 11, 1975): 130-33. Leslie Gelb, "Pact with Soviet on Missile Curb Reported in Peril," NYT, October 15, 1975.

4. Selective Counterforce Targeting, 1974-1976

Some five weeks before SALT II was scheduled to resume in February 1974, Secretary of Defense James Schlesinger formally announced a significant change in America's strategic doctrine. In a January 10 address to the Overseas Writers Club, Schlesinger revealed that the United States had begun the process of improving the accuracy of U.S. missile forces in order to achieve "counter-force options" vis-à-vis potential adversaries. He noted:

> There has taken place a change in the strategies of the United States with regard to the hypothetical deployment of the central strategic forces. A change in targeting strategy...[to give the president] an option to hit a different set of targets--military targets...beyond an all-out nuclear attack against cities.[1]

Schlesinger subsequently shed some light on the reasoning behind this change in American strategy in the administration's Fiscal Year 1975 Posture Statement:

> Threats against allied forces...demand more limited responses than destroying cities. Nuclear threats to our strategic forces, whether limited or large-scale, might well call for an option to respond in kind against the attacker's military forces.... To the extent that we have selective response options--smaller and more precisely focused than in the past--we should be able to deter such challenges. But if deterrence fails, we may be able to bring all but the largest nuclear conflicts to a rapid conclusion before cities are struck. Damage may thus be limited and further escalation avoided.[2]

In his Posture Statement, Secretary Schlesinger suggested that there were at least two different sets of questions involved in the change in American strategic doctrine. First, there was the matter of adding flexibility to our war plans.

Second, there was the issue of improving our counterforce capabilities.[3]

ADDED FLEXIBILITY

At the time of his January 10 speech and in a subsequent press conference on January 24, Secretary Schlesinger attempted to leave the impression that an American policy of limited nuclear options was novel and that the existing strategic doctrine of mutual assured destruction--deterrence by having the capability of enduring an enemy's first strike and subsequently inflicting unacceptable damage on the enemy[4]--lacked the capacity for flexible options. President Nixon, in fact, had implicitly struck the same theme when in his 1970 "State of the World" message he had rhetorically posed the question: "Should a President, in the event of a nuclear attack, be left with the single option of ordering the mass destruction of enemy civilians, in the face of the certainty that it would be followed by the mass slaughter of Americans?"[5] Nixon returned to this theme a year later when he noted in his 1971 "State of the World" message that "I must not be--and my successors must not be--limited to the indiscriminate mass destruction of enemy civilians as the sole possible response to challenges. It would be inconsistent with the political meaning of sufficiency to base our force planning on some theoretical capability to inflict casualties presumed to be unacceptable to the other side."[6]

Contrary to the impression conveyed by these statements, postwar U.S. nuclear targeting policy has always included military targets; and, as one author has noted, pre-1974 Nixon administration targeting plans included five "options" plus various sub-options, with U.S. attacks to proceed along the following spectrum: (1) Soviet strategic retaliatory forces (e.g., missile sites, bomber bases, submarine bases); (2) Soviet air defenses away from cities (e.g., those covering U.S. bomber routes); (3) Soviet air defenses near cities; (4) Soviet command and control centers and systems; (5) if necessary, all-out "spasm" attack. Sub-options included such things as the use of clean/dirty bombs, air/ground burst weapons, larger/smaller warheads, civil defense/evacuation.[7] However, it is true that "not until the Nixon administration did a few individuals finally take the initiative to build consensus within the bureaucracy on the need to change the actual plans for the use of American nuclear weapons" and to develop and explicate publicly the rationale for a "flexible options" policy.[8]

In this regard, the first bureaucratic step to change official American targeting plans, i.e., to alter the Single Integrated Operational Plan (SIOP), was undertaken within the Defense Department soon after the conclusion of the SALT I accords. Prior to mid-1972, the Pentagon's Office of Systems Analysis had made an extensive study of the SIOP and concluded it was too rigid, but this study and its conclusions were confined to the level of intra-office discussion until after the initialing of the SALT I agreements.[9] Soon thereafter, however, in July 1972 the Defense Department formally established an intra-agency group, chaired by chief Pentagon researcher John Foster, to study possible revisions in the SIOP. By the end of 1972, this group completed its study and unequivocally recommended a number of specific changes in the SIOP's preplanned attacks.

At that point, during the early days of the second Nixon administration, the Foster group's recommendations were passed on to an inter-agency committee, composed of representatives of the Department of Defense, Department of State, the Arms Control and Disarmament Agency, the Central Intelligence Agency, and the National Security Council. By the summer of 1973, the inter-agency committee had reviewed and, in essence, ratified the Defense Department group's conclusions and recommendations. So, by mid-1973, the intellectual foundation for a revised strategic doctrine had been formally agreed to by the bureaucracy and in the next few months it was ratified by officials at the highest levels of the executive branch. Consequently, by late 1973-early 1974 American employment policy on targeting flexibility, which describes targets and how the United States government plans to use the nuclear weapons it possesses currently and American declaratory policy, which gives guidance to U.S. officials on what to say publicly about employment and weapons acquisition policies, were ready to be brought into line publicly.[10]

In the Fiscal Year 1975 Posture Statement, the principal measures which Secretary Schlesinger proposed to achieve greater targeting flexibility included: (1) improvment of command and control arrangements and (2) improvment in the accuracy of some of our warheads.[11] On the matter of improving our command and control arrangements, Schlesinger specifically had in mind the development of the so-called Command Data Buffer System. The system, if installed, would enable the Strategic Air Command to make rapid targeting changes beyond those stored in the missile guidance systems, electronically transmitting retargeting data to the missile from its launch center. In specific terms, the installation of this system would allow SAC to change a target tape on a missile in roughly thirty-six minutes from the launch control center, whereas in the past it took SAC between sixteen and twenty-four hours to change a target tape on a missile and then it was still necessary to enter the missile in the silo to change the tape.[12]

In testimony before the Senate on the Command Data Buffer System, Schlesinger declared that "when you get down to the hard rock of [this sort of] flexibility in targeting plans, there really is very little criticism of that. Across the entire spectrum of people who have thought about this issue, there is relatively little criticism."[13] On this point, Schlesinger proved to be right, at least insofar as criticsm of this system by the Congress.[14] Indeed, in the Spring of 1974, when the Senate Foreign Relations Subcommittee on Arms Control held hearings to examine the administration's plans to change our strategic doctrine, the chairman of the subcommittee, Edmund Muskie, began the hearings by stating in his opening remarks that "I feel certain that there are few, if any, Members of Congress who doubt the desirability of improving our command and control systems."[15] And in the course of subsequent congressional consideration of the administration's Fiscal Year 1975 budget request, there was, in fact, virtually unanimous support in both the Senate and the House for full funding of programs to improve our command and control systems.

IMPROVED ACCURACY AND COUNTERFORCE

On the matter of improving the accuracy of some of our warheads and, in general, of developing a more effective counterforce capability, reaction in the Senate was less uniformly supportive of the administration's plans than it had been toward improvement in our command and control systems. For Senator Henry Jackson and many of his colleagues on the Armed Services Committee, the decision to improve our counterforce capabilities was long overdue.[16] However, to a number of other senators--most notably Brooke, Case, Humphrey, Kennedy, Mathias, McIntyre, Mondale, and Muskie--the development of a more effective counterforce capability represented a significant and potentially unwise change in U.S. strategic policy. These and other senators were apprehensive about both the short- and long-term implications of the proposed changes in our targeting capability and about the overall program costs of developing the kind of counterforce capability that Secretary Schlesinger seemed to envisage.

In addition, these senators wondered whether the proposed changes in our strategic doctrine reflected a change in the longstanding U.S. policy of avoiding development of the kind of counterforce capability which the Soviets could perceive as having a first-strike potential. This policy, they recalled, had been a cardinal tenet of U.S. strategic thinking during both the 1960s and early 1970s. Indeed, in 1969, in response to an inquiry from Senator Brooke, President Nixon had seen fit to state publicly that "the purpose of our strategic program is to maintain our deterrent, not to threaten any nation with a first strike," and affirmed that the United States does "not intend to develop counterforce capabilities which the Soviets could construe as having a first-strike potential."[17] In October 1971, during the Senate's debate on the

Fiscal Year 1972 Military Procurement Authorization Bill, the administration reaffirmed its anti-counterforce stance when it openly opposed three amendments offered by Senator James Buckley which were intended to increase the counterforce capability of the Minuteman III and Poseidon missiles. At the time, the administration publicly proclaimed that it "cannot support the proposed amendments. It is the position of the United States to not develop a weapon system whose deployment could reasonably be construed by the Soviets as having a first-strike capability. Such a deployment might provide an incentive for the Soviets to strike first."[18]

Besides issuing these public statements, the executive branch had tacitly agreed to tie the non-development of an effective counterforce program with a first-strike potential to further progress at SALT. At the time of Senate consideration of the SALT I accords, Senators Edward Brooke and Harold Hughes offered an amendment to the legislation ratifying the SALT I Interim Agreement which stipulated that the conclusion of a more comprehensive strategic arms limitation agreement would be "dependent upon preservation of the long-standing United States policy that neither the Soviet Union nor the United States should seek unilateral advantage by developing a first-strike potential."[19] Subsequently, the executive branch made it clear that this amendment was consistent with administration policy, and it was accepted unanimously by the Senate. This U.S. policy of non-development of a threatening counterforce capability was once again reaffirmed by James Schlesinger at his confirmation hearings to be Secretary of Defense in June 1973.[20] By early 1974, following Schlesinger's pronouncements about the need for the United States to improve the accuracy of some of our warheads and to develop an improved counterforce capability, there was a good deal of concern about the meaning and possible implications of the proposed selective counterforce targeting doctrine.

In a letter sent to Secretary Schlesinger a few days after his January 10 speech to the Overseas Writers Club, Senator Brooke spelled out his concerns "over possible provocative and destabilizing implications of contemplated changes in the U.S. strategic doctrine." In the letter, Brooke explicitly raised the question of whether the position of the United States had changed on the matter of counterforce and first-strike disarming capability.[21]

On Friday, January 25, 1974, soon after the receipt of the Brooke letter, Secretary Schlesinger had breakfast with the Massachusetts senator at the Pentagon to discuss the administration's proposed changes in U.S. targeting doctrine. The Defense Secretary assured Brooke that the United States did not seek to develop its new counterforce programs so as to have a disarming first-strike capability, and he explained in general terms what the new targeting doctrine was intended to achieve. Schlesinger, however, declined to answer in detail the senator's questions about what quantitative and qualitative criteria would determine "adequate strategic nuclear flexibility" or how the administration's new targeting doctrine might affect the U.S.-Soviet nuclear balance and progress at SALT II. Schlesinger declared that he preferred to answer these and related questions in a detailed written reply.[22]

Some two weeks later, on February 10, 1974, Schlesinger sent Senator Brooke a one-page letter. In it, Schlesinger once again declined to answer in detail any of the specific questions which Brooke had raised. The Defense Secretary did suggest, however, that:

> ...a serious national debate should take place about all questions associated with the strategic forces of the U.S. and U.S.S.R..... I believe the specific answers to your questions will come out in the testimony [before Congress], and so I would like to limit myself to a more general response here in order that there not be an inordinate and inaccurate unilateral focus on the question of accuracy itself as some sort of overriding key to deterrence or to the stability of the strategic balance.[23]

Predictably, Senator Brooke was unhappy about Schlesinger's refusal to answer his queries--either in person or, as promised--in written reply. After initially criticizing the Defense Secretary for his unwillingness to "provide a classified and unclassified response to each of my questions," Brooke went on to say:

> ...it is self-evident that the issues involved here are far too important for the continued security of the American people to be decided by the Administration alone on narrow technical grounds. Therefore, I am heartened by your commitment to a "serious debate" on the strategic question.[24]

Brooke added, "I will certainly insist that this take place."[25]

Like Brooke, Senator Edmund Muskie was also very concerned about the possible implications of the administration's proposed changes in our targeting doctrine. On February 4, Muskie convened a closed-door meeting of his Arms Control Subcommittee with CIA Director William Colby to discuss American and Soviet strategic forces. Muskie and several other senators at the subcommittee hearing questioned Colby closely about recent press reports of a major Soviet strategic build-up and about the relative strength and deterrent value of the two sides during the period from 1974 up to the time when the Interim Agreement was due to expire in 1977. Several senators expressed particular interest in the accuracy and throw-weight of the Soviets' strategic forces and in Soviet counterforce capabilities in general. Other senators explored with Colby America's capacity to monitor future Soviet counterforce developments and deployments, particularly regarding MIRVs. Muskie, among others, queried the CIA Director at length about what deficiencies in our nuclear forces would be overcome by the implementation of Schlesinger's proposed changes in our counterforce capabilities.

Colby's responses supported the idea of a recent Soviet military build-up and, concomitantly, the need for the United States to improve its counterforce capabilities. More specifically, at this meeting, Colby described in detail the characteristics and potential capabilities of the systems which the Soviets had begun developing since the conclusion of SALT I--several new land-based ICBMs (SS-16, SS-17, SS-18, SS-19, SS-20); a new Delta-class missile firing submarine; and a still larger class of missile-launching submarine, which would carry more than the twelve-missile load of the Delta. The Colby hearing, however, was more of an intelligence briefing for a group of relatively uninformed senators than it was a probing discussion of the policy implications of America's adoption of a selective counterforce targeting policy.

Accordingly, following the meeting with Colby, Senators Muskie and Case decided to invite Secretary Schlesinger to appear before the Arms Control Subcommittee to discuss in detail the implications of the Defense Secretary's proposed changes in our strategic doctrine. In correspondence with Schlesinger prior to the hearing, the two senators explained the interest of subcommittee members in the following way:

> We hope to discuss in some detail current United States and Soviet strategic weapons programs and policies. The Members [of the subcommittee] are particularly interested in new developments in U.S. strategic programs and policies, such as the decision to retarget some Minuteman missiles and to develop more accurate warheads. We would like to know how these changes will affect the relative strategic position of the two sides during the next several years, whether these moves might be interpreted by the Russians as an American attempt to achieve a one-strike potential, and what might be the impact of these new programs and policies upon efforts to bring about strategic arms limitations and reductions.[26]

Soon after receipt of this correspondence, Schlesinger, eager to discuss publicly with Congress the assumptions, processes, and weapons systems associated with our SALT policy and underlying strategic doctrine, accepted the subcommittee's invitation to appear.[27] The hearing was set for March 4, 1974.

At the hearing, Schlesinger was accompanied by five associates from the Pentagon, and Benson Adams, a member of the State Department's Office of Political-Military Affairs. Senators Muskie and Case were joined in the questioning of the witnesses by Senators Fulbright, Symington, Pell, Humphrey, Aiken, and Percy. The hearing, which lasted for more than three hours, took place behind closed doors. However, at Senator Muskie's request and with Secretary Schlesinger's concurrence, the transcript of the hearing was released to the public in early April 1974, after being "sanitized" by the executive branch. At one point in the hearing, Muskie observed that "if we have some of this discussion today in the public record, it could be the basis for a more sophisticated level of debate on strategic defense issues."[28] Secretary Schlesinger agreed. The publicly-released transcript provided the most detailed explanation of the executive's thinking about selective counterforce targeting in particular and current U.S. nuclear strategy in general then available.

At various points in the March 4 hearing, Secretary Schlesinger endeavored to point out that the administration did not wish to develop the kind of counterforce capability that would threaten the Soviets. Indeed, he repeatedly underscored the fact that there "is just no possibility that a high confidence disarming first-strike is attainable for either side."[29] He argued that the accuracy and yield improvements in our warheads that the administration sought would make possible more "efficient" and "discriminating" use of our forces against both soft and hard targets and that this was a far cry from developing the kind of counterforce capability that might be construed as having first-strike potential.[30]

For Schlesinger, the primary rationale for the proposed improvements in our counterforce capabilities was to enhance American deterrent strength. As Schlesinger explained in his opening remarks to the subcommittee,

> The purpose of the change...is to shore up deterrence. We believe...that the change in targeting doctrine serves to shore up deterrence across the entire spectrum of risk and consequently reduces the likelihood, which is fortunately already very low, of any outbreak of nuclear war. We want to keep recourse to nuclear weapons as far away as possible.... We are using the strategic forces... to establish a framework within which conflict, if it comes, would be fought at a low level, in terms of the violence of the weapons involved....[31]

To elaborate on this general point, Schlesinger then outlined a likely scenario in which an improved U.S. counterforce capability would enhance deterrence. Schlesinger explained:

> If the United States were to strike at the urban industrial base of the Soviet Union, the Soviet Union could and presumably would fire back, destroying the urban industrial base of the United States. Consequently, the

> Soviet Union, under those circumstances, might believe
> that the United States would be self-deterred from making
> use of its strategic forces. Thus, they might regard
> themselves as relatively risk-free if our deterrent
> doctrine...were to stress only going against cities.[32]

Hence, for Schlesinger, more flexibility and accuracy in our strategic forces would enhance deterrence.

In the course of the hearing, Schlesinger made a number of other strategic points in behalf of the proposed weapons improvements. Foremost among these was the argument that improvement in the accuracy of our warheads would significantly reduce unintended civilian damage in the event of a limited nuclear exchange and, in more general terms, would help bring American forces into "essential equivalence" with those of the Soviet Union. As 1973 wore on and the Soviets began to develop several different MIRVed systems, Schlesinger explained, he and others in the administration became increasingly concerned about the numerical and throw-weight advantages permitted the Soviet Union under the terms of the SALT I accords. While not arguing for exact parity with the Soviets in terms of all of the major indices of strategic power (i.e., numbers of warheads, delivery vehicles, accuracy, throw-weight, reliability, and megatonnage), Schlesinger and other key executive branch officials did stress that the United States should maintain, in the interest of world peace, strategic forces not significantly inferior to those of the Soviets in numbers, throw-weight, or counterforce capability. Thus in early 1974, the beginning of new research and development programs in the counterforce area, they reasoned, would send a signal to the Soviet Union that the United States was not going to allow the Soviets to develop even the appearance of "marked superiority" in the counterforce area.[33]

In sending such a signal, according to Schlesinger, the United States hoped to accomplish at least three objectives. First, America hoped to persuade the Soviets not to continue the expansion of their counterforce programs, implying that we would do whatever was necessary to match whatever new systems they developed. In the graphically blunt words of General George Brown, then Air Force Chief of Staff and currently Chairman of the Joint Chiefs of Staff, "if the Soviets insist on an arms race, there will be an arms race."[34] Second, this policy was designed to dissuade the Soviets from exploiting the full potential of a major counterforce capability. On this point, one knowledgeable observer has explained that the executive's logic ran as follows:

> If the Soviets were to contemplate knocking out the U.S.
> ICBM force in the first phase of a nuclear conflict, an
> American President should not be left only with the op-
> tion of threatened retaliation against Soviet cities;

rather, he should have the counterforce option of depriving the Soviets of their ICBM forces also, so that both sides would be 'even.' Faced with this prospect, the Soviets would not be tempted to call on their counterforce capability, and would thus remain deterred.[35]

The third objective of this policy was related to SALT. Since the conclusion of the SALT I accord in mid-1972, as has been noted previously,[36] SALT had been at an impasse. In early 1974, Schlesinger, Pentagon SALT representative Paul Nitze, and others felt that the American announcement of an intention to develop a selective counterforce capability would reduce the temptation to the Soviets to continue on the same two-pronged path they seemed to have been following since 1972: on the one hand, moving ahead in a major way with development of their offensive weapons systems, and on the other hand, refusing to negotiate seriously at the talks in Geneva. In short, it was hoped that the publicly-announced change in U.S. policy regarding counterforce would persuade the Soviets to talk seriously about a joint scaling down of more advanced offensive weapons programs and to come to some agreement at SALT II.[37]

The reaction of most members of the Arms Control Subcommittee to Schlesinger's testimony was generally skeptical. Senators Case, Humphrey, and Muskie were, seemingly, the most apprehensive about the proposed changes in our strategic policy. These senators feared that U.S. development of more accurate and higher yield warheads might be perceived by the Soviet Union as a threat to its hardened missiles and hence the survivability of its retaliatory forces. And while Secretary Schlesinger had continually disavowed any administration intention to develop "a major counterforce capability," these senators feared that going ahead with the improved accuracy and yield programs the Defense Secretary proposed would raise the spectre of a possible American first-strike capability and in so doing greatly undermine the U.S.-Soviet nuclear balance.[38]

An allied concern on the part of these and other subcommittee members was whether the proposed changes in our strategic policy would significantly lower the nuclear threshold by making nuclear weapons seem more useable in the form of precision nuclear strikes (or even using highly accurate missiles with conventional explosives). Theretofore, the employment of nuclear weapons in any manner had been considered an "acceptable" policy option by the president in only the most dire circumstances, and there was concern among several senators that any significant improvement in our counterforce capabilities would make the use of nuclear weapons more "respectable."[39]

Another concern among several subcommittee members was the likely effect these proposed new programs would have on the prospects for an early conclusion of a SALT II accord. While Schlesinger was confident that the new counterforce research and development programs would give the Soviets additional incentives to move ahead at SALT, Case, Humphrey, and Muskie believed that beginning the proposed new programs would have exactly the opposite effect on the strategic arms talks. These senators felt that in light of the 1974 U.S. advantage over the Soviets in terms of weapons accuracy, the Soviets, in response to the initiation of new American counterforce programs, would likely speed up—rather than negotiate away—their incipient MIRV programs. This, it was feared, would not only destabilize the world's nuclear balance but also seriously impair the emerging détente between the United States and the Soviet Union.[40]

Additionally, these senators feared that funding research and development on new counterforce programs might well repeat the administration's experience with MIRVs. Initially intended to be a bargaining chip at SALT, i.e., a system proposed in order to be bargained away in subsequent negotiations, the MIRV program took on a bureaucratic and political momentum of its own that became very difficult for either side to halt.[41] The same outcome was feared regarding the new counterforce programs if they were initially approved, even if only in the research and development stage.[42]

The final major concern among members of the subcommittee related to the possible cost of these new programs. At various times during the March 4 hearing, Secretary Schlesinger reiterated the point that the proposed changes in our strategic policies would not necessitate the expenditure of any new monies. As Schlesinger emphasized, these programs were related to adding "flexibility," not "sizing," to our nuclear forces.[43]

On the other hand, $77 million was contained in the Fiscal Year 1975 defense request for new research and development to improve U.S. counterforce capabilities. Of this amount, $25 million was requested to increase the yield of a new Mark 12A warhead for Minuteman III missiles, $20 million was requested to improve the guidance system for Minuteman IIIs, and $32 million was asked for research on a new and potentially very accurate maneuverable warhead with a terminal guidance system (MARV). These expenditures were obviously only a small fraction of the $21.9 billion contained in the military procurement authorization bill. But there was serious concern among several senators that these Fiscal Year 1975 expenditures represented a watershed in terms of U.S.-Soviet counterforce weapons rivalry and that if pursued in full, the cost of developing these weapons would likely mushroom to the level of billions of dollars when the programs under consideration moved from research and development to the production and deployment stages.[44]

During the spring of 1974, while the Foreign Relations Subcommittee on Arms Control was holding a series of hearings on the political implications of Secretary Schlesinger's proposed changes in our strategic doctrine, the Armed Services Subcommittee on Research and Development was holding in-depth hearings on the research and development programs contained in the Fiscal Year 1975 defense budget request. In all, more than ninety-one hours of public hearings were held by the subcommittee on some thirty-seven new research and development programs requested by the administration. Among these programs, the $77 million contained in the bill to improve our counterforce capabilities came under extensive scrutiny; and after hearing several days of testimony by executive branch officials and other witnesses, on May 7, 1974 the subcommittee, led by its chairman Thomas McIntyre, decided to refuse funding for these programs by a vote of 3-2. Paralleling the thinking of several Arms Control Subcommittee members, a majority of the Research and Development Subcommittee held that improved accuracy was not necessary to preserve the security of the American nuclear deterrent and that such projects might well be counter-productive by accelerating the pace of Soviet offensive weapon development. At the same time it disapproved the $77 million in the bill designed to improve our counterforce programs, the subcommittee approved a series of U.S. development projects aimed at increasing the survivability of the U.S. retaliatory force. These included monies for air- and sea-launched cruise missiles and air- and land-based mobile missiles.[45]

Some three weeks later, the full Armed Services Committee reversed the subcommittee's judgment on the three counterforce programs contained in the Fiscal Year 1975 Military Procurement Authorization Bill and by a 15-2 vote,[46] voted to fund fully the administration's $77 million counterforce request. However, in the Armed Services Committee's report to the full Senate on the bill, it was noted that the United States should avoid "any combination of forces that could be taken as an effort to acquire the ability to execute a first-strike disarming attack against the U.S.S.R." The committee also withheld a decision on deployment of programs to improve our counterforce capabilities and expressed hope that SALT II might soon make progress in restraining the development of counterforce weapons.[47]

Before the Fiscal Year 1975 Military Procurement Authorization Bill reached the Senate floor for debate, a concerted effort was made by several senators to ascertain the views of Secretary of State Kissinger with regard to the foreign policy implications of the proposed counterforce programs. In February 1974, at the same time that Secretary Schlesinger was invited to appear before the Arms Control Subcommittee, Senators Muskie and Case asked Secretary Kissinger to testify on U.S. strategic policy. Although Kissinger indicated in private conversations with Muskie that he would welcome the opportunity to testify on this subject before the Arms Control Subcommittee, no such hearing could be scheduled with Kissinger's staff. As in the case of SALT II, Kissinger, on the one hand, professed an active interest in testifying before the Senate on U.S. strategic policy but, at the same time, was in practice unwilling to do so.[48]

Frustrated by the inability of their Foreign Relations Committee colleagues to have Kissinger testify before Congress on strategic issues and apprehensive about the potential implications of Congress' funding the proposed counterforce programs, Senators Mondale, McIntyre, and Mathias sent the Secretary of State a formal letter on May 22, 1974. In the letter the three senators noted:

> Substantial concern has been expressed that these [counterforce] programs have important and adverse implications for our relationship with the Soviet Union and for strategic stability. From the standpoint of your responsibilities for our foreign relations as well as your professional expertise on strategic issues, we would appreciate your views on:
> —whether these programs will contribute to stability in a crisis or increase the premium for a a first strike;
> —whether these programs will contribute to the survivability of our deterrent forces;
> —whether these programs can be controlled in SALT and effectively monitored by national means by the Soviet Union;
> —whether these programs will contribute to détente, to the easing of tensions, or whether they will call into question our intentions and thereby exacerbate relations with the Soviet Union.[49]

The letter concluded by stating that "your response to this letter will be particularly useful before the Senate acts upon the Military Procurement Authorization Bill." None of the senators ever received a response to this letter.

Accordingly, when the Secretary of State appeared on June 7, 1974 before the full Foreign Relations Committee to testify on the Fiscal Year 1975 Foreign Aid Authorization Bill, Senator Muskie seized the occasion to ascertain Kissinger's views on the foreign policy implications of the improvement of our counterforce capabilities. In response to Muskie's questions, Kissinger urged committee members to support the administration's $77 million request. The Secretary of State explained:

> I do not oppose particular improvements in our strategic forces especially at a time when the Soviet Union is engaged in a rapid improvement of its strategic forces and before there has been a conclusion of the current phase of the SALT negotiations.... In terms of national strat-

egy however, I do not believe that...a counterforce strategy is one on which the country can rely as one of its principal tools.... I make a distinction between discriminating targeting which also requires accuracy and counterforce strategy which involves a first strike against the existing proposed retaliatory force, which, therefore, must have a character of massiveness and overwhelming threat which cannot but fuel measures on the other side.... So I would make a distinction between these two elements.[50]

Kissinger then broke off his generalized discussion of counterforce strategy by indicating that "I would prefer to go into the entire subject in a more comprehensive way" and declaring that he looked forward to participating in subsequent Arms Control Subcommittee hearings on U.S. strategic policy.[51] Although such hearings were held in 1974, 1975, and 1976 before both the Foreign Relations Arms Control Subcommittee and the Armed Services Research and Development Subcommittee, Kissinger's participation was never forthcoming.

On June 10, 1974, about two weeks after the Armed Services Committee had completed action on the Fiscal Year 1975 Military Procurement Authorization Bill, the full Senate considered that part of the bill dealing with counterforce weaponry. Prior to this, a series of meetings was held in early June among staff members working for the senators on the Foreign Relations and Armed Services Committees who were most skeptical of the counterforce programs. At the staff level, it was concluded that if an amendment were to be offered on the Senate floor to delete the $77 million for counterforce programs contained in the Military Procurement Authorization Bill, it would stand a reasonable chance of success. It was also concluded that the possibility of passing such an amendment would be significantly enhanced if the amendment were offered by a member of the Foreign Relations Committee and argued for in terms of the adverse foreign policy consequences that would likely result from the improvement of our counterforce capabilities at this time. Implicit in this second conclusion was the judgment that given the overwhelming Armed Services Committee recommendation to fund these programs, the full Senate would not be likely to turn down monies for improving the accuracy and yield of our warheads on strictly strategic grounds. It might do so, however, if a case were made for how these programs would significantly impair the prospects for a new SALT agreement and threaten the détente relationship between the United States and the Soviet Union.

To the consternation of several Senate staffers, no member of the Foreign Relations Committee was willing to offer an amendment on the floor to delete the counterforce program monies in the Fiscal Year 1975 defense budget. Although they indicated to their staffs that they were opposed to these programs and would speak out against and vote against monies for them, several Foreign Relations Committee members were unwilling "to take on Senators Jackson and Tower" on this issue. Despite the Arms Control Subcommittee hearings that had been held during the spring of 1974 on U.S. nuclear strategy, these Foreign Relations Committee members felt uneasy and unsure of themselves challenging the judgment of members of the Armed Services Committee on such a complex strategic issue as counterforce. The argument that the counterforce question was not purely a military issue but a foreign relations one as well was not sufficiently convincing to compel any member of the Foreign Relations Committee to lead a floor fight against the proposed counterforce programs.

Ultimately, Senator McIntyre, Chairman of the Armed Services Subcommittee on Research and Development, and Senator Brooke, a former member of the Armed Services Committee, jointly offered an amendment on the Senate floor concerning the proposed counterforce programs. The McIntyre-Brooke amendment stipulated that no monies should be spent for these programs until the president had submitted a report to the Congress which concluded that it was impossible to get an agreement with the Soviet Union to limit the development of MIRVs.

Before calling for a rollcall vote on this amendment, Senator McIntyre convened the Senate in an infrequent closed-door session to present secret information on the accuracy and vulnerability of our strategic forces. In this session, McIntyre argued that our present ICBMs "were sufficiently accurate to attack military bases as well as cities and that, even with the Soviet missile developments, the Minuteman would be invulnerable for the foreseeable future."[52] Senators Jackson, Stennis, and Tower countered McIntyre's presentation with many of the same strategic arguments Secretary Schlesinger had presented to the Senate in committee testimony earlier in the spring.

Following the two-hour closed-door session, the Senate went into open session to debate the amendment. Most of the same arguments on both sides of the amendment were repeated publicly. In both the closed and open session, the debate centered on the strategic pros and cons of improving our counterforce weaponry, with Senator Stennis at one point tellingly observing that as a quail hunter "accuracy is always to be desired in a weapon" and at another time describing the executive branch's request as "just another field where we are improving our weapons."[53] In the end, proponents of selective counterforce targeting like Stennis prevailed, and the Senate voted by 48-37 to reject the McIntyre-Brooke amendment.[54] Following the debate and vote, however, Senator Brooke commented to a colleague: "This was the kind of debate we should have on all strategic issues but rarely do."[55]

One of the basic assumptions underlying the administration's doctrinal shift on the use and development of counterforce weaponry was the belief that nuclear exchanges limited to military targets would result in relatively few civilian casualties. In an article in the October 1973 issue of Foreign Affairs, Wolfgang Panofsky challenged that assumption and criticized in detail the Defense Department's method of calculating civilian casualties resulting from limited nuclear exchanges.[56] Having read the Panofsky article and seen the Congress approve full funding for the administration's counterforce weapons programs for Fiscal Year 1975, Senator Case wrote Secretary Schlesinger on July 2, 1974 asking for a briefing on "your estimates of the total casualties and destruction expected to result from so-called nuclear 'counterforce attacks' against military installations in the United States." In his request for the information, Case expressed the hope that "these estimates would encompass the full range of consequences to the United States population and society."[57]

The briefing was set for July 23. However, from mid-July staff communications with the Defense Department, Case learned that the briefing was to be principally concerned with estimates of destruction directly resulting from blast and fallout, and that the Pentagon considered "anti-military attacks" to be so small in scope that their effects would be, in essence, localized and not susceptible to analysis of their larger societal consequences.[58]

This displeased Case, for he was convinced that "anti-military" exchanges, once initiated, could include a large number of military targets on either side and would have large-scale societal consequences. Accordingly, Case cancelled the July 23 meeting and wrote Secretary Schlesinger a three-page letter on July 25, requesting a "comprehensive" briefing on the entire range of consequences resulting from limited nuclear exchanges. In this second letter to Secretary Schlesinger, Case listed some of the kinds of estimates which he wished to have included in the briefing (e.g., casualties to civilian as well as military personnel from blast, fallout, fire, damage to food supplies, contamination of land and water, et al.).[59]

Pursuant to Schlesinger's receipt of Case's July 25 letter, an August 14 briefing was arranged for Senator Case with Terence King of the Office of the Secretary of Defense and William Kaufman, a consultant to the Secretary of Defense. The briefing was to include discussion of the Pentagon's assessment of the full range of destruction and casualties that would result from nuclear attacks against American military installations. From Case's point of view, the briefing was highly "unsatisfactory" because of the seemingly "superficial" way that the Defense Department chose to calculate the effects of limited nuclear exchanges. Indeed, it was particularly "galling" to Case that at the same time the executive branch was urging significant changes in U.S. targeting doctrine, it was not making any systematic effort to assess the assumptions and possible ramifications associated with the proposed changes.[60]

Immediately after the Kaufman-King briefing, Case wrote to Senator Muskie recommending that the Arms Control Subcommittee convene a hearing with Secretary Schlesinger "to present the casualty estimates now available and to describe the analytical effort now underway to develop a more comprehensive understanding of the consequences of limited nuclear exchanges." In his letter to Muskie, Case added that "since it is likely that the Defense Department will request continued funding of weapons designed to fight a 'counterforce' war, I think it incumbent upon us to examine all of the consequences of the change in strategy involved."[61]

Muskie fully concurred in this judgment, and an Arms Control Subcommittee meeting with Secretary Schlesinger on counterforce attacks was arranged for September 11, 1974. Senators Muskie, Symington, Pell, Case, Javits, and Pearson took part in the hearing. In his opening remarks to the subcommittee, Schlesinger mentioned the fact that in 1968 the Preparedness Subcommittee of the Armed Services Committee had expressed interest in America's developing such a capability. In response to this, Senator Stuart Symington, a long-time member of both the Armed Services Preparedness Subcommittee and the Foreign Relations Arms Control Subcommittee, spoke out on the "vitally important" role of the current hearings in regard to "our future, our economy, and our defense posture." Symington added that "I would much rather have what you think as a former head of the AEC and present Secretary of Defense than I would anything we [senators] discussed in 1968; because in those days we were very ignorant about nuclear weapons."[62]

Not surprisingly, many of the substantive points Schlesinger made in defense of selective counterforce targeting were the same ones he had made in the earlier March 4 hearing. At the September hearing, though, the emphasis of his remarks was on the potential "damage-limiting" effect of such targeting. When pressed by Senator Case to discuss the executive branch's estimates of "not only direct casualties from blast and fallout but also the indirect casualties from man-years lost, the amount of land that would be lost [and] the psychological impact" resulting from limited nuclear exchanges, Schlesinger estimated that fatalities from a Soviet attack against the bases of U.S. ICBMs would range from 800,000 to three million people. Schlesinger admitted, though, that the administration's studies on casualties and destruction resulting from such an attack were not yet fully completed and would have to be submitted to the Congress subsequently.[63]

More so than in earlier testimony, perhaps reflecting the administration's frustration with the continuing impasse at SALT, Schlesinger emphasized in the September 11 hearing the link between the administration's counterforce plans and the Soviet Union's strategic policies. At one point, when asked about the relationship between the executive's publicly-announced intention to improve our counterforce capabilities and the role of bargaining chips in the strategic arms limitation talks, Secretary Schlesinger responded:

> I would like to broaden the concept of the bargaining chip. What I am saying is that there must be a functional relationship between the forces the Soviet Union deploys; that they must recognize that if they take certain steps we will match them; and that, therefore, we have R&D projects in development which will give us the capability to respond to certain actions of the Soviet Union which we hope they will not take. If they do take these actions then these projects will not be bargaining chips. We think we must be prepared to deploy these additional capabilities in order to maintain an appropriate balance, but we are prepared to renounce them if the other side reciprocates. We would hope they turned out to be bargaining chips and that both sides are willing to renounce their new programs.[64]

And later in the hearing, when pressed by Senators Javits and Muskie to make public a "sanitized" transcript of the briefing, Schlesinger responded he would be happy to do so--for the educational benefit of Congress, the American public, and leadership of the Soviet Union. Regarding the Soviets, Schlesinger declared that "they must see in the realities of our force structure, our planning and our resolve a high degree of certainty that they will elicit a response from us that they would prefer to avoid. That is the heart of deterrence and they must see it."[65]

On September 12, 1974, the day following the Arms Control Subcommittee hearing with Secretary Schlesinger, Senators Muskie and Case sent Senator Fulbright, Chairman of the Foreign Relations Committee, a letter suggesting that the committee try to gain an "independent judgment" on the adequacy of the Defense Department's forthcoming studies on casualties and destruction resulting from limited nuclear exchanges. Specifically, Muskie and Case wanted to get Fulbright's support for a request for assistance from the Congressional Office of Technology Assessment (OTA). The two ranking members of the Arms Control Subcommittee proposed that OTA be asked by the Foreign Relations Committee to assemble "a competent and unbiased panel of experts" to: (1) "conduct a critical review of current DOD estimates of casualties and damages expected to result from nuclear attacks upon military installations in the United States" and (2) "identify deficiencies and limitations of existing and planned analyses and, where indicated, develop and carry out independent analyses to provide the Congress with a comprehensive and independent understanding of the full consequences of nuclear attacks against military installations in the United States."[66]

Fulbright, sympathetic to the arguments of Muskie and Case, then wrote Senator Edward Kennedy, Chairman of the Technology Assessment Board, on behalf of the Foreign Relations Committee. In his letter Fulbright requested that OTA conduct the kind of "review and analysis" called for in the Muskie-Case letter of September 12, a copy of which he forwarded to Kennedy. Fulbright also expressed the belief that a "review and analysis of the accuracy of Department of Defense estimates of the potential effects of limited warfare upon United States society, with the results made available to the public, could help achieve a better understanding of these important strategic issues."[67]

Upon receipt of Fulbright's letter, Kennedy had OTA convene a panel of experts to evaluate the Defense Department's estimates of the potential effects of limited nuclear war upon American society. The panel, which was chaired by Jerome Wiesner, President of the Massachusetts Institute of Technology, and consisting of several other prominent scientists, completed its report in late February 1975. The panel concluded, among other things, that the Defense Department's casualty figures were substantially too low for the attacks in question due to a lack of attention paid to the intermediate and long-term effects of atomic fallout from a nuclear attack.[68] The panel explained that the Department of Defense's studies "did not adequately reflect the large uncertainties inherent in any attempt to determine the civilian damage which might result from a nuclear attack" and suggested that the Pentagon review its analyses using more "realistic assumptions."[69]

As a result of the OTA panel's criticisms, which were transmitted by the Foreign Relations Committee to Secretary Schlesinger in late winter 1975, the Defense Department reexamined its calculations and conclusions, and on July 11, 1975 the Pentagon submitted new estimates to the committee on the number of civilian casualties that would result from a Soviet strike against military bases in the United States. In the revised estimates, which were made public by the Foreign Relations Committee on September 16, 1975, the Pentagon calculated that between 3.5 million and 22 million people would die from such a Soviet attack. The Pentagon added, moreover, that "the most representative scenario" for all-out attack on all U.S. strategic nuclear facilities was 6.7 million fatalities.[70]

In a statement issued at a September 1975 Arms Control Subcommittee hearing to discuss with three members of the OTA panel the effects of limited nuclear warfare, Senator Symington, then chairman of the subcommittee, remarked that the Pentagon's "new estimates give a much clearer picture of the possible costs to our citizenry of these so-called 'limited' attacks against our military targets." Symington added, "What we have found so far is only the beginning of what we need to learn about the costs of nuclear war. Perhaps we sometimes lose sight of the unprecedented and truly terrible costs of [such] war."[71]

Symington's statement was, in significant part, misleading. For the Senate had had all of the new information available to it earlier that summer when it had approved the administration's Fiscal Year 1976 defense request, including more than $109 million for the continuing development of counterforce weaponry. At the time the Fiscal Year 1976 Military Procurement Authorization Bill was brought to the Senate floor in early June 1975, Senator McIntyre offered an amendment to the bill, much as he had done the year before, to delete all of the counterforce program monies in the legislation. As chairman of the Armed Services Research and Development Subcommittee, McIntyre had recently been given a copy of the new Pentagon estimates. At the time, he believed that sharing this information with his colleagues would lead to the termination of the counterforce programs.

On June 4, 1975, McIntyre convened a secret session of the Senate in which the New Hampshire senator disclosed the new Pentagon estimates. To counter McIntyre's secret information on fatalities, Senator Jackson produced theretofore secret information about the increasingly rapid Soviet build-up of its counterforce programs.[72] The debate between McIntyre and Jackson continued in a subsequent public session. In the end, the argument that the United States needed these new programs to match the Soviets' build-up and to spur progress at SALT based on the Vladivostok Accords carried the day. The McIntyre amendment was defeated 52-42.[73]

Senate opponents of counterforce, however, achieved a minor victory two days later when the Senate approved by a 43-41 vote an amendment offered by Hubert Humphrey to prohibit flight testing of the MARV system unless the president certified to Congress that the Soviet Union was also testing MARVs. As Humphrey explained in the floor debate, once the MARV had been flight tested, there would be no way to verify whether or not it had been deployed.[74] Earlier, the House had defeated a similar MARV amendment by a 276-124 vote; when the issue reached the Senate-House conference in mid-June 1975, the Senate prohibition was dropped. The Senate-House Conference Report subsequently explained that the "Senate conferees agreed to recede" from the MARV amendment "but only after they determined that no MARV testing would be concluded during the Fiscal Year 1976."[75]

In the Fiscal Year 1977 Military Procurement Authorization Bill, the administration, for the third year in a row, asked for an increasingly large amount of money for the improvement of U.S. counterforce capabilities. Specifically, in Fiscal Year 1977, the administration asked for not only research and development monies for various command and control and higher accuracy and yield programs, but also for authority to begin production of the new Mark 12A warheads. This warhead, a key element in the administration's counterforce plans for precision nuclear strikes, carries three independently targetable warheads with considerably more accuracy than any warheads the United States currently has in place on our missiles.

Once again, the Armed Services Research and Development Subcommittee held extensive hearings on the administration's request and probed possible policy alternatives to those proposed by the executive branch. Following a series of hearings, the subcommittee and, subsequently, the full committee approved the executive's request. But when the bill reached the floor, Senators Kennedy and Cranston decided to offer modifying legislation. Making many of the same arguments on the Senate floor in opposition to counterforce that Senator McIntyre and others had done the past two years, they offered an amendment to delete $317 million from the bill for the procurement of sixty Minuteman III ICBMs and for equipping the new missiles with the Mark 12A warhead. In the end, the arguments of Kennedy and Cranston were rejected on May 25, 1976 by a 49-35 vote after several hours of debate.

A SUMMING UP

Senate involvement in the process by which the U.S. policy of selective counterforce targeting was established was, in many ways, significantly more meaningful than legislative involvement had been during either SALT I or SALT II. Concerning counterforce targeting, the Senate as a whole, various Senate committees and subcommittees, and a relatively large number of individual senators all attempted to become informed about the details of proposed U.S. policy. At various times during the 1974-76 period, administration officials were pressed by senators individually or in subcommittee to explain in detail and defend American policy, the bases underlying that policy, and the appropriations requested thereunder. In addition, largely through the activities of the Arms Control Subcommittee of the Foreign Relations Committee and the Research and Development Subcommittee of the Armed Services Committee, debate inside and outside the Senate on U.S. counterforce policy and alternatives to that policy was considerable. In addition, in 1974-75, a basic assumption underlying the executive branch's position was challenged, and the responsible officials were held accountable by the Senate for miscalculations concerning the number of civilian casualties that would result from a Soviet strike against military bases in the United States.

In the end, the executive branch's Fiscal Year 1975,

1976, and 1977 requests for monies to support a policy of selective counterforce targeting were approved by Congress. However, the involvement of the Senate in the process by which U.S. policy was made was perceptively different from that during either SALT I or SALT II. Regarding selective counterforce targeting, the Senate did not passively support the executive's proposals but actively debated, questioned, and challenged them.

NOTES

1. Remarks of James Schlesinger to the Overseas Writers Club, January 10, 1974.
2. Report of the Secretary of Defense to the Congress on FY 1975 Defense Budget, March 4, 1974 (Washington: Government Printing Office, 1974), p. 38.
3. Ibid., pp. 26, 30, 44. Also, see Thomas Wolf, The SALT Experience: Its Impact on U.S. and Soviet Strategic Policy and Decisionmaking, The Rand Corporation, Report R-1686-PR (September 1975), p. 122.
4. Such damage has been estimated as 75 million fatalities and between 50 and 75 per cent of a nation's industrial capacity. See Barry Carter, "Nuclear Strategy and Nuclear Weapons," Scientific American 230, no. 5 (May 1974): 23-24.
5. U.S. Foreign Policy for the 1970's, February 18, 1970, p. 122.
6. Ibid., February 25, 1971, pp. 170-71.
7. Desmond Ball, Déja Vu: The Return to Counterforce in the Nixon Administration, California Seminar on Arms Control and Foreign Policy (December 1974), pp. 10-12. Also, see Henry Rowen, "Formulating Strategic Doctrine," in Appendices to the Commission on the Organization of the Government for the Conduct of Foreign Policy, Vol. 5 (June 1975), pp. 225-32.
8. Lynn Davis, Limited Nuclear Options: Deterrence and the New American Doctrine, Adelphi Paper Number 121 (London: IISS), p. 3.
9. In fact, several other initiatives had been undertaken within the government to change the SIOP prior to the conclusion of the SALT I accords in May 1972. But these had little operational consequence. Confidential Interview.
10. Confidential Interviews. See also Davis, pp. 3-4.
11. Report of the Secretary of Defense to the Congress on the FY 1975 Defense Budget, p. 38.
12. For a detailed discussion of the Command Data Buffer System, see "Briefing on Counterforce Attacks by Secretary James Schlesinger, September 11, 1974," Hearing before the Subcommittee on Arms Control, Committee on Foreign Relations, 93rd Congress, 2d Session (Washington: Government Printing Office, 1975), pp. 21-22. Also, see Drew Middleton, "U.S. is Bolstering Nuclear Force to Survive Attack and then Destroy

Enemy," NYT, April 15, 1976.

13. "Hearing on U.S.-U.S.S.R. Strategic Policies, March 4, 1974, before the Subcommittee on Arms Control, Committee on Foreign Relations," U.S. Senate, 93rd Congress, 2d Session (Washington: Government Printing Office, 1974), p. 10.

14. Some members of the arms control community in the United States were, in fact, critical of Schlesinger's proposed improvements in our command and control arrangements on the grounds that these improvements, inter alia, would make nuclear war more thinkable and therefore more likely. See, for example, Herbert Scoville, Jr., "Flexible MADness?" Foreign Policy 14 (Spring 1974): 175-76.

15. "Opening Statement of Senator Edmund Muskie, April 4, 1974," Hearing on U.S. Nuclear Strategy before the Subcommittee on Arms Control, Committee on Foreign Relations, U.S. Senate, 93rd Congress, 2d Session.

16. See "Address by Senator Henry Jackson before the Military Committee on NATO," reprinted in Aviation Week and Space Technology, December 11, 1972, pp. 53-55.

17. See Congressional Record, July 29, 1970.

18. Ibid., October 5, 1971.

19. See Strategic Arms Limitation Talks: Legislative History of the Jackson Amendment, 1972.

20. See "Hearings on the Nomination of James Schlesinger to be Secretary of Defense before the Committee on Armed Services," U.S. Senate, 93rd Congress, 1st Session, June 18, 1973, pp. 61-62.

21. See "Brooke Meets with Schlesinger on Possible Alterations in U.S. Strategic Policy," Press Release from the Office of Senator Edward Brooke, January 26, 1974.

22. Confidential Interview.

23. Letter from James Schlesinger to Senator Edward Brooke, February 7, 1974.

24. Letter from Edward Brooke to James Schlesinger, February 10, 1974.

25. Ibid. It should be noted that in mid-January 1974, Senator Brooke had also sent a letter to Secretary Kissinger, querying the Secretary of State on several points about how the proposed changes in our targeting policies would affect SALT. Kissinger never responded to the Brooke letter. Confidential Interview.

26. Letter from Senators Edmund Muskie and Clifford Case to James Schlesinger, February 28, 1974.

27. For a detailed description of Schlesinger's views in support of open discussion with Congress on U.S. strategic policy, see Aerospace Daily, February 22, 1973, p. 24.

28. Hearing on U.S.-U.S.S.R. Strategic Policies, March 4, 1974, before the Subcommittee on Arms Control, Committee on Foreign Relations, U.S. Senate, 93rd Congress, 2d Session (Washington: Government Printing Office, 1974), p. 42.

29. Ibid., p. 38.

30. Ibid., pp. 36-41.
31. Ibid., p. 7.
32. Ibid., p. 8.
33. Ibid., pp. 10, 18.
34. "If the Soviets Insist, There Will Be an Arms Race" (Interview with General George Brown), U.S. News and World Report, February 25, 1974, p. 63.
35. Thomas Wolfe, The SALT Experience, p. 129.
36. See Chapter 3, pp. 54-55.
37. Hearing on U.S.-U.S.S.R. Strategic Policies, March 4, 1974, pp. 10-24.
38. Ibid., pp. 18-19.
39. Ibid., pp. 14, 34-35, 42-43, 55. Also, see John Baker and Robert Berman, "Evaluating Counterforce Strategy," NYT, February 22, 1974.
40. Hearing on U.S.-U.S.S.R. Strategic Policies, March 4, 1974, pp. 21, 35-36, 39-40, 52.
41. See Ted Greenwood, Making the MIRV: A Study of Defense Decision Making (Cambridge: Ballinger, 1975), Chap. 3.
42. Hearing on U.S.-U.S.S.R. Strategic Policies, March 4, 1974, pp. 37-38.
43. Ibid., pp. 8, 38.
44. Alton Frye has estimated that $1.5 billion will be required to complete development of a new re-entry vehicle and warhead, and that between $5 billion and $6 billion will be required to install such payloads on all of the 550 Minuteman III ICBMs scheduled for deployment. See A Responsible Congress, pp. 93-94. For a detailed analysis of the projected long-range costs of improving our counterforce capabilities, see William Kincade and John Baker, "U.S. Strategic Doctrine: Nuclear Warfighting versus Nuclear Deterrent Capabilities," A Background Paper prepared by Members of Congress for Peace Through Law, February 12, 1974, pp. 7-13.
45. WP, May 8, 1974.
46. The two senators who continued to vote against monies for the counterforce programs in the bill were McIntyre and Hughes. Senator Harry Byrd voted with McIntyre and Hughes within the subcommittee but reversed his vote in full committee.
47. "Report of the Committee on Armed Services, U.S. Senate on Authorizing Appropriations for Fiscal Year 1975 for Military Procurement, Research and Development, and for Other Purposes," Report Number 93-884, May 29, 1974, pp. 20-24. The individual views of Senators McIntyre and Hughes are contained on pp. 181-90 of the report.
48. See Chapter 3, pp. 55-56.
49. Letter from Senators Walter Mondale, Thomas McIntyre, and Charles Mathias to Secretary Henry Kissinger, May 22, 1974.
50. "Transcript of Hearing on the FY 1975 Foreign Aid Authorization Bill, June 7, 1974," before the Committee on Foreign Relations, U.S. Senate, 93rd Congress, 2d Session.
51. Ibid.

52. NYT, June 11, 1974.
53. Congressional Record, June 10, 1974.
54. In the House, consideration of the proposed counterforce programs was relatively pro forma. On May 22, 1974, Representative Bella Abzug introduced an amendment to the FY 1975 Military Procurement Authorization Bill to delete $225 million from eight research and development programs, including the three programs covered by the McIntyre amendment. After a short debate, the House overwhelmingly rejected the Abzug amendment.
55. Confidential Interview.
56. See "The U.S.-Soviet Mutual Hostage Relationship," pp. 109-18.
57. Letter from Senator Clifford Case to James Schlesinger, July 2, 1974.
58. Confidential Interview.
59. Letter from Senator Clifford Case to James Schlesinger, July 25, 1974.
60. Confidential Interview.
61. Letter from Senator Clifford Case to Senator Edmund Muskie, August 14, 1974.
62. "Briefing on Counterforce Attacks, September 11, 1974," Hearing before the Subcommittee on Arms Control, Committee on Foreign Relations, U.S. Senate, 93rd Congress, 2d Session (Washington: Government Printing Office, 1975), p. 25.
63. Ibid., pp. 25-29.
64. Ibid., p. 41.
65. Ibid., p. 47.
66. Letter from Senators Edmund Muskie and Clifford Case to Senator J. William Fulbright, September 12, 1974.
67. Letter from Senator J. William Fulbright to Senator Edward Kennedy, September 19, 1974.
68. See Sidney Drell and Frank von Hippel, "Limited Nuclear War," Scientific American 235 (November 1976):27-37.
69. "Analyses of Effects of Limited Nuclear Warfare," a Report Prepared for the Subcommittee on Arms Control, Committee on Foreign Relations, 94th Congress, 1st Session, September 1975 (Washington: Government Printing Office, 1975), pp. 4-12.
70. Ibid., p. 11.
71. "Statement of Senator Stuart Symington on the Effects of Limited Nuclear Warfare," September 17, 1975. Also, see "Hearing of the Effects of Limited Nuclear Warfare, September 1975," before the Subcommittee on Arms Control, Committee on Foreign Relations, 94th Congress, 1st Session (Washington: Government Printing Office, 1976).
72. Confidential Interview. Also, see Leslie Gelb, "The Changing Estimates of Nuclear Horror," NYT, October 19, 1975.
73. See Congressional Record, June 4, 1975.
74. Ibid., June 6, 1975.
75. Senate Report 94-334, July 26, 1975. Also, see

"Limited Nuclear War: Sane or Suicidal?" _Congressional Quarterly_, August 9, 1975, pp. 1747-1748.

5. Conclusion

How does one account for the Senate being relatively more meaningfully involved in the making of selective counterforce targeting policy in 1974-76 than in the setting of policy for either SALT I or SALT II during the 1969-76 period? To answer this question, it is necessary to examine the attitude, organization, and mode of operation of both the executive branch and the Senate during these years.

It is no secret that the foreign and defense policy-making processes of both the Nixon and Ford administrations were shaped to a significant extent by one man, Henry Kissinger. Early in 1969, with President Nixon's concurrence, Kissinger established a complex, closed system to formulate U.S. policy for the strategic arms limitation talks. The decision-making machinery that was set up allowed the president's Assistant for National Security Affairs to define the shape of the issues being considered by the government; to specify what alternatives existed; and, ultimately, to present choices to the president for his decision. The most unusual characteristic of this policy-making process was not that the ultimate decisions were made privately by the president based on alternative choices presented by his National Security Assistant. This had generally been the case in previous administrations. What was unique under the Kissinger-created system was that the shape of the issues under discussion at the highest policy-making levels was often kept secret from much of the government, including most of the executive branch and generally all of Congress. Put another way, under the SALT policy-making process established by Kissinger during the 1969-76 years, many of those normally responsible for shaping and debating an issue--whether in the executive branch or legislative branch--were often not able to identify alternative considerations or the grounds on which choices were made.[1]

In part, this highly centralized, closed policy-making system was instituted to minimize potentially damaging leaks of information. In part, it was created to maximize Henry Kissinger's influence on presidential decisions. In part, too, it reflected the distaste of Kissinger--and seemingly Presidents Nixon and Ford--for extensive intra-executive, congressional or public discussion of U.S. SALT policy. In August 1969, Kissinger explained his feelings on the subject in the following way:

> If you see two people playing chess and someone comes along and says, 'Why don't you make this move?', you're in an impossible position. You can't answer. You can't tell your chess opponent your game plan. This attempt may involve 15 or 18 moves. Critics, perfectly legitimately, raise questions. But we're in the difficult position of not being able to answer.[2]

In significant part as a result of Kissinger's negativism toward congressional or public discussion of SALT issues, the Senate was never able to develop a satisfactory arrangement for consultation on SALT policy during the 1969-76 years. For much of this period, the two executive officials best suited to consult with the Senate on SALT policy matters were Kissinger and Gerard Smith. Yet, with neither was a modus vivendi ever worked out for meaningful executive-legislative consultation. As Assistant to the President for National Security Affairs during the January 1969-September 1973 period, Kissinger saw fit to invoke executive privilege whenever invited to testify before the Congress on strategic arms policy as well as other issues.[3] This was the case despite the fact that Kissinger was chairman of the SALT Verification Panel and the administration's chief SALT policy-maker in these years. During the September 1973-December 1976 period when he was Secretary of State, Kissinger testified on many issues before the Congress, but was, in fact, not willing to appear on the subject of U.S. strategic arms policy. In the words of one former high-ranking official, "Kissinger counted on his own expertise, persuasiveness and charisma to push through any SALT agreement that might be negotiated. Accordingly, he never felt the need to consult Congress on SALT."[4]

Concerning Smith, chief SALT negotiator and ACDA Director, the problem of consultation with Congress was more complicated. Until 1970, Smith was "not permitted by the White House to brief the Foreign Relations Committee."[5] After "permission" was granted to Smith to appear before the Congress, serious problems arose about the value of his testimony. This was not due to the lack of availability as was the case with Kissinger. Indeed, during the 1970-72 years, Smith testified some thirty times before various interested congressional committees.[6] Rather, the problem related to the nature of his testimony. Smith was under strict instructions not to discuss with Congress the critical issues under debate within the executive branch concerning SALT. As Lawrence Weiler, Counselor to Smith's Arms Control and Disarmament Agency during the 1969-72 years, has since pointed out about executive branch testimony before the Congress regarding matters like SALT:

> When spokesmen operate under what are, in effect, White House instructions to avoid serious discussion of most of the issues under debate in the executive branch and not to volunteer explanation of details of positions that would reveal the real positions of an administration, there can be little real collaboration [with Congress] in developing national policies. Nor can there be under such a system an honest exchange between government and citizen.[7]

White House limitations on his testimony constituted only one problem concerning Smith's consultation with Congress. Another related to Smith's knowledge of various critical elements of the SALT negotiations. As John Newhouse has described in some detail,[8] at critical junctures in the SALT I negotiations-- for example, the five months prior to the May 20, 1971 U.S.- U.S.S.R. joint statement on SALT or the four days Kissinger spent in Moscow in April 1972 working out limits on submarines-- Smith and his colleagues on the U.S. negotiating team were unaware of the Nixon administration's "back-channel" talks with the Soviets. Yet, these efforts, shielded from virtually all of the U.S. governmental bureaucracy and all of Congress, were critically related to the evolution of the American position at SALT and, ultimately, the successful conclusion of the SALT I accords. As Newhouse has summarily noted in this regard, "Kissinger kept fully informed only his constituency of one."[9] Clearly, there was a limit to the ability of Smith (and his successor as chief SALT negotiator, U. Alexis Johnson) to keep the Senate fully informed about U.S. SALT policy, even in the absence of special instructions from the White House.

In sum, executive-Senate consultation regarding SALT during the 1969-76 years was characterized by:

- -<u>pro forma</u>, reportorial briefings, generally by Gerard Smith, of the Foreign Relations and Armed Services Committees;

- -the executive branch's general unwillingness to share with the Senate the critical details of the basic proposals of the U.S. government;

- -the executive branch's unwillingness to show the texts of the U.S. proposals to the Senate;

- -the executive branch's disinclination to keep the Senate informed about changes in U.S. positions during the course of the negotiations;

- -an overall mode of operation on the part of the executive branch designed to thwart Senate interest in discussing and debating, in either public or secret meetings, various policy issues involved in the negotiations, including Soviet counter-proposals.[10]

This pattern of executive-Senate interaction was designed to control carefully the flow of SALT information between the two branches of government, and it did this. As a direct result, the administration exercised a good deal of control over the SALT policy process. To the extent that information on SALT was given to the Senate during the 1969-76 years, it was done so in a highly selective, frequently self-serving, manner. That is, information was generally released at an executive-determined time and typically included only those items and arguments supportive of the administration's position. This often had its intended effect--co-opting or shoring up legislative support for a particular policy stance. However, it also had the effect of generally cutting the executive branch off from independent advice and counsel from the Senate, and in overall terms, it clearly put the legislative branch, either uninformed or poorly informed, at a considerable disadvantage vis-à-vis the executive branch in the SALT decision-making process.[11]

To be sure an examination of executive branch attitudes and operational patterns regarding consultation provides only a partial explanation for the lack of meaningful Senate involvement in the SALT policy process in the 1969-76 period. One must also look at the Senate itself. For had a number of senators (or representatives), either individually or collectively, frontally challenged the executive branch concerning the virtual exclusion of Congress from the policy-making process, the system's closed nature might well have been modified. But the overwhelming majority of senators opted not to do this. Some felt that formulating U.S. policy for arms negotiations with foreign countries was an "executive" responsibility that belonged exclusively to the executive branch and to the president in his role as Commander-in-Chief. These senators felt that involvement of the legislative branch in the SALT policy-making process would constitute unwise "outside" interference in negotiations where the president knows best and might well jeopardize a favorable outcome. Others believed that it was impossible for Congress to participate actively in setting U.S. policy for on-going negotiations and felt they would have ample opportunity to form an opinion and present their views after the executive branch had concluded an agreement and submitted it to Congress for approval. Still other members felt that they and the available staff resources--whether congressional or nongovernmental--lacked the background and expertise to enable the legislative branch to make a useful contribution in this complex area of policy. As Congressman Les Aspin has explained:

Almost every Congressman feels that he is an expert on

education, or economics or any number of domestic issues. But when it comes to defense, most Congressman lack confidence, and so they turn to 'experts.' To most Congressmen defense experts are people in uniform, not academics in universities or 'think-tanks.' Uniforms equal expertise, and the higher the rank, the greater the expert.[12]

Perhaps most importantly, virtually no member of Congress felt compelling constituent pressure to play a more active role in the SALT process. In his book on Congress, David Mayhew has perceptively noted that the overriding goal of all members of Congress is to be re-elected.[13] During the 1969-76 years, there was little electoral incentive for any senator to be actively involved in the SALT policy process. On the contrary, almost all senators felt pressure to focus their attention on matters of higher political salience and more immediate urgency to their constituents, such as U.S. policy in Indochina or economic conditions within the United States. Most senators fully expected that if the SALT negotiations were successful, it would be possible to share some of the credit, and if the talks resulted in failure or in an inequitable agreement, it would be possible to apportion virtually the entire blame to the executive branch.

These predilections of individual senators were reinforced by a lack of leadership in the Senate committee directly charged with overseeing U.S. foreign policy--the Foreign Relations Committee. Given the seventeen clauses of the Constitution that specify the Senate's foreign affairs power, the Foreign Relations Committee potentially has enormous authority in all aspects of American foreign policy. As one observer has noted:

> Foreign policy implications of the common defense, treaties, presidential appointees to carry out foreign policy, and money matters in support of external efforts are referred to the Committee before the full Senate offers its advice and consent or dissent. Therein lies the special nature of the Committee, but its importance goes beyond its Constitutionality. This is expressed by the esteem in which it is held within the Senate....[14]

The Foreign Relations Committee, chaired by J. William Fulbright during the 1969-74 period and John Sparkman since 1975, was disinclined, however, to participate actively in the SALT policy-making process during the 1969-76 years.[15] In general terms, Chairmen Fulbright and Sparkman viewed the role of the Foreign Relations Committee to be that of an educational forum, not as a legislative entity organized to affect U.S. policy directly. Committee involvement in U.S. policy toward Indochina was a stark exception, not the rule. A former Committee staff member has since commented that:

Fulbright ran the committee as though foreign policy were
too complicated to be left to the mere amateurs in the
Senate. He saw his job as assisting the professionals in
the White House and the State Department.[16]

Fulbright, himself, shed further light on the operation of the
Foreign Relations Committee under his chairmanship when in a
colloquy on the Senate floor in 1969, he revealingly remarked:

> The Foreign Relations Committee is more of a committee to
> influence the attitudes and policies of the State Depart-
> ment than it is to legislate[sic]. It is not legislative
> in the sense of an appropriations committee, which actually
> makes an allocation of dollars. Its functions are quite
> different from the major functions of a legislative com-
> mittee. For example, in dealing with a treaty, how would
> a treaty be allocated?[17]

Consequently, during the 1969-76 years, different views
about SALT were aired only irregularly through hearings of the
Foreign Relations Committee and, more commonly, the Arms Control Subcommittee. However, these hearings generally were
one-sided, pro forma executive presentations to a few passive,
largely uninformed senators. Indeed, it was common practice at
these hearings for the executive to present faits accomplis to
the Congress and for committee members, in turn, to applaud
passively the executive's initiatives and not to add any new
ideas or even to protest congressional exclusion from the process during which policies were hammered out. The chairman as
well as the committee members, with few exceptions, did not
press the administration for information beyond what was provided and did not have the motivation to try to affect directly
U.S. SALT policy--either at these hearings or through the confirmation hearings of such key SALT officials as Henry Kissinger, James Schlesinger, U. Alexis Johnson, or Fred Iklé.

To the extent that the committee took up legislation relating to SALT, it was, without exception, in the form of non-
binding Sense-of-the-Senate Resolutions. These resolutions
were frequently introduced by non-committee members (e.g.,
Brooke, Cranston, Kennedy, Mathias, Mondale) and referred to
the Foreign Relations Committee for its consideration. In most
cases, these non-binding expressions of legislative sentiment
died within the committee. And on those rare occasions when
Chairman Fulbright or Sparkman or the various Arms Control Subcommittee chairmen--Gore, Muskie, Symington--held hearings on
the given resolution and the full committee subsequently approved the legislation by formal vote, the executive branch
typically disregarded the advisory opinion conveyed in the legislation, and the committee did not challenge the executive's actions. Indeed, on one occasion in 1970, President Nixon went so
far as to say publicly that a resolution approved by both the

committee and the entire Senate concerning limiting MIRVs was "irrelevant" to U.S. SALT policy and nary a word of protest was heard from any committee members.[18]

Sense-of-the-Senate resolutions are not the way to make policy. A basic element of congressional power is legislating--law-making is policy-making. Most of the members of the Foreign Relations Committee well understood this. Yet, under the chairmanship of Senator Fulbright and Senator Sparkman, the committee considered only Sense-of-the-Senate resolutions regarding SALT, rather than any binding legislation. Upset with Fulbright's view of the committee as an educational forum rather than a legislative organ, former committee member Gale McGee once lamented:

> The Senate's role in foreign policy in the future can best be achieved by deeds rather than by words--and least of all by the Sense-of-the-Senate resolution. The role of the Foreign Relations Committee in the policy process is whatever it decides to be. Thus, the committee can hide behind the shelter of congressional resolutions, or it can stand on its deeds.[19]

Less content with executive predominance of the SALT policy-making process was the Senate Armed Services Committee, particularly its Subcommittee on Arms Control (known as the Subcommittee on SALT before 1973), chaired by Henry Jackson. At various times during both the Nixon and Ford administrations, Jackson and other Armed Services Committee members like Chairman John Stennis, Research and Development Subcommittee Chairman Thomas McIntyre, Sam Nunn, and John Tower, aided by a technically expert staff, actively endeavored to play an influential role in the SALT process. At various times, hearings were held on the military implications of issues and weapons systems being negotiated at SALT. Also in the 1974-76 years, there were several hearings on possible Soviet violations of the terms of the SALT I accords. On other occasions, executive branch witnesses were pressed to explain U.S. strategic arms policy, including the bases and premises underlying our negotiating posture. And through an amendment to the legislation ratifying the 1972 SALT I Interim Agreement, Senator Jackson tried to set the parameters within which future strategic arms limitation talks would take place. In practice, however, these efforts, while worth noting, were of only marginal significance vis-á-vis policy, save the Jackson amendment. For, during the 1969-76 years, the involvement and influence of Armed Services Committee members regarding U.S. SALT policy were significantly restricted by Henry Kissinger's unwillingness to appear before this or any other committee to provide detailed information about SALT; the Nixon and Ford administration's highly closed policy-making process, with no one other than Kissinger really able to brief the committee on SALT; and the Armed Services

Committee's lack of jurisdiction over treaties and ambassadorial nominations.

Concerning Senate participation in the setting of U.S. selective counterforce targeting policy, many of the above-noted considerations did not pertain. For one thing, there was not the same legitimacy question. On the issue of counterforce targeting policy which required appropriations for the policy to be implemented, the Senate's active participation in the policy process was mandated by the Constitution--both in Article 1 which gives Congress the power of the purse and in Articles 12, 13, and 14, which respectively give Congress the power 'to raise and support armies,' 'to provide and maintain a navy,' and 'to make rules for the government and regulation of land and naval forces.'

Indeed, with the Constitution as justification, both the Senate and the House of Representatives in recent years have significantly increased the number of items in the executive branch's defense request which have to pass through two stages in each chamber annually: first, authorization by the Senate and House Armed Services Committee; second, appropriation by the relevant subcommittees of the appropriations committees. This now includes all funding for research, development, test, and evaluation; personnel strengths of the Reserves and for each part of the Armed Forces; and procurement of aircraft, missiles, naval vessels, heavy torpedos, and combat vehicles. In addition, all appropriations for weapons must now fit underneath the annual ceiling set for all defense expenditures by the Senate and House Budget Committees created in 1975.

Put another way, to implement the administration's planned changes in our targeting doctrine, the executive branch was not able to institute and maintain the kind of closed policy-making system that it had set up for SALT. Here, the legislative branch had greater potential and more direct leverage for influencing policy. To gain the appropriations needed for the improvement of our counterforce weapons capabilities in Fiscal Years 1975, 1976, and 1977, the executive branch was forced to provide to the Senate a good deal of information about the proposed policy changes, to explain in detail the underlying bases for the administration's proposals, and to defend in both open and closed sessions its weapons proposals as compared to alternatives put forward by members of the Senate. In short, if the executive branch wanted the requisite funds for developing an improved counterforce capability, it had no choice but to engage in lengthy, in-depth, give-and-take interchanges with the responsible Senate committees and subcommittees, to whom it had necessarily to provide a significant amount of operative policy information.

Of course, to say that the executive branch had to provide detailed information to the Senate and testify on its counterforce weapons proposals is not to say that the Senate would necessarily scrutinize closely or challenge the executive branch's proposals. Indeed, as was evident during the period from 1945 until the 1969 ABM debate, the authorization and appropriation processes did not ensure active congressional participation in the policy-making process for various weapons systems because the authorization and appropriations processes and congressional committee hearings can be merely formalized procedures for rubber-stamping executive branch initiatives. The fact that there was active Senate participation in the setting of U.S. counterforce targeting policy during the 1974-76 years must be attributed to at least two additional factors: (1) the widespread congressional consensus in the post-ABM period about the propriety and constitutional authority for the Congress to scrutinize carefully weapons requests, particularly given increasingly common cost over-runs and rising concern for keeping down budgetary deficits and (2) an aggressive and probing Armed Services Subcommittee on Research and Development, led by Thomas McIntyre and a highly professional technical staff, which had jurisdiction over the counterforce weapons requests.

From the preceding analysis of Senate involvement in SALT I, SALT II, and selective counterforce targeting policy, what can be said about future congressional involvement in the strategic arms policy process, given the Senate's performance in this policy area during the 1969-76 years? The most salient lesson to be drawn from the preceding case studies is that when money is directly involved in the establishment of a given strategic arms policy--that is, when the executive branch needs appropriations from Congress to set policy--it is considerably more likely that the legislative branch will be provided with a significant amount of detailed, operative policy information and will play an active role in the policy process than in cases in which the link between appropriations and policy is less direct or clear. Put another way, in cases where policies can not be carried out without appropriations, the legislative branch has its greatest leverage potential vis-á-vis executive policy initiatives. This is not to suggest that in all cases in which appropriations are requested by the executive branch to pursue a given strategic arms policy Congress will meaningfully help shape policy. Indeed, in the overwhelming majority of cases, Congress has not been an active participant in this policy area during the postwar period. However, it is true that in cases in which monies are directly requested by the executive branch to establish a given strategic arms policy--such as in the case of selective counterforce targeting--several factors frequently pertain that make meaningful congressional involvement more likely than in other cases in this arcane area of public policy.[20]

Among these factors are the following:

(1) Several different congressional committees (e.g.,

Armed Services, Appropriations, Budget) are necessarily involved in an institutional way in the policy process when appropriations are requested.

(2) Members of Congress perceive a certain legitimacy in their involvement in the policy process when appropriations are requested.

(3) Members of Congress are not generally defensive about their lack of expertise when forced to vote on appropriation requests.

(4) Members of Congress are frequently motivated to challenge executive branch arguments when monies are involved.

(5) Members of Congress often perceive electoral stakes being directly involved in appropriation matters, given the generally high constituent interest in budgetary matters.

(6) The executive branch is more forthcoming in providing information, of necessity having to appear before responsible congressional committees and subcommittees to justify the given appropriations request.

On the other hand, in cases in which the executive branch does not directly request appropriations to pursue a given strategic arms policy--such as in setting the U.S. negotiating posture at SALT--many of the exact opposite considerations pertain. And in these instances, particularly when the executive branch is loath to provide detailed policy information to Congress, it is frequently the case that the legislative branch does not play an active role in the policy process.

A SUMMING UP

Legislative and executive branch attitudes and patterns of operation tend to be different regarding strategic arms policies that directly require appropriations for their implementation and those that do not. To be sure, if individual members of Congress strive to be actively involved in the setting of U.S. SALT policy--policy which does not generally require appropriations directly for implementation--they can, on occasion, play a significant role in the policy process. The involvement of Senator Henry Jackson in the SALT process demonstrates this. But the real point concerning Senator Jackson or others like Senators Case, Humphrey, Kennedy, McIntyre, or Muskie is that their involvement in the SALT policy process during the 1969-76 years was perceptibly different from the involvement of the Senate in the selective counterforce targeting policy-making process during the 1974-76 years. Concerning SALT, the relatively few senators interested in the details of the issues tried to involve themselves in the policy process through occasional secret briefings, sporadic public hearings, and infrequent promulgation of non-binding Sense-of-the-Senate resolutions. Given the executive branch's disregard for these advisory resolutions, its disinclination to share detailed SALT information with the Senate, and disinterest on the part of the overwhelming majority of senators toward strategic arms policy, Senate influence on U.S. SALT policy was marginal.

It has been argued by some students of the legislative process that Congress frequently makes its influence felt on the executive branch in the arms control and defense area by indirection rather than through direct involvement. That is, the legislative branch affects policy by discouraging the executive branch from following certain policy courses for fear of incurring the wrath of Congress. In some cases, the exertion of congressional influence indirectly may be significant. But in the cases of SALT I and SALT II during the 1969-76 period, the overwhelming evidence suggests that with the exception of the Jackson amendment to SALT I--and it concerned SALT II-- the Senate did not play a particularly meaningful role in the policy process.

By contrast, in the case of selective counterforce targeting, the Senate was actively and meaningfully involved in the setting of U.S. policy. In the end, both the Senate and the House ratified the executive branch's counterforce initiatives during the 1974-76 years. But before doing so, through a series of Senate committee hearings on authorizations for the proposed programs, through additional hearings on the implications of counterforce targeting policy, and through extended debate on the Senate floor on legislation authorizing monies to implement the proposed policy, individual senators, responsible committees, as well as the Senate as a collective body actively debated, questioned, challenged, and helped shape policy.

In any case, in the future, the Senate's role in the setting of policy for both SALT and strategic weapons requests is likely to grow. As staff resources on strategic arms policy issues grow in both qualitative and quantitative terms; as senators as a result become more informed about and comfortable with the complexities associated with these issues and correspondingly demand more information from the executive branch; as constituents increase the pressure on their elected representatives to spend tax dollars more prudently, including those spent on defense, increased Senate participation in various aspects of the strategic arms policy-making process becomes inevitable. This development should not be viewed as either unhealthy or undesirable, for an activist legislative branch can and should play a central role in formulating this country's strategic arms policies.

NOTES

1. For a detailed discussion of the Kissinger-created, closed decision-making system regarding SALT, see Graham Allison, An Overview to the Commission on the Organization of the Government for the Conduct of Foreign Policy (Washington: Government Printing Office, 1975), pp. 76-79. Also, see Raymond Garthoff, "Negotiating with the Russians: Some Lessons from SALT," International Security 1, no. 4 (Spring 1977): 3-24 and Roger Morris, Uncertain Greatness: Henry Kissinger and American Foreign Policy (New York: Harper and Row, 1977), pp. 208-12.

2. Quoted in James Nathan and James Oliver, United States Foreign Policy and World Order (Boston: Little, Brown and Co., 1976), p. 561.

3. It should be noted that during the 1969-73 period, Kissinger did meet privately from time to time with individual senators to discuss SALT. However, these meetings were irregular, off-the-record, and generally convened to shore up congressional support for already decided-upon executive branch policy. Confidential Interview.

4. Confidential Interview. In a seminar at Stanford University on April 2, 1976, Helmut Sonnenfeldt, a long-time Kissinger aide, echoed his former boss' view about the necessity of on-going consultation with the Congress when he remarked: "It is important that we pursue SALT II negotiations now and we will deal with Congress and ratification when the time comes."

5. Francis Wilcox, Congress, the Executive and Foreign Policy (New York: Harper and Row, 1971), p. 53. Confidential Interview.

6. "Hearings on the Strategic Arms Limitation Agreements" before the Committee on Foreign Relations, United States Senate, 92nd Congress, 2nd Session, June-July 1972 (Washington: Government Printing Office, 1972), p. 22. Also, see John Lehman, The Executive, Congress and Foreign Policy (New York: Praeger, 1976).

7. The Arms Race, Secret Negotiations and the Congress, p. 11.

8. See Cold Dawn, pp. 203-205, 229-30, 243-44.

9. Ibid., p. 203.

10. Confidential Interview. Also, see Weiler, pp. 13-15.

11. For an excellent discussion of the role that information plays in the policy process, see John Murphy, "Knowledge is Power: Foreign Policy and Information Interchange Among Congress, the Executive Branch, and the Public," Tulane Law Review 49, no. 3 (March 1975). For a discussion of the key role information played in the 1969 ABM debate, see Anne Cahn, Congress, the Military, and Information (Beverly Hills, California: Sage Publications, #04-017, 1974).

12. Quoted in Anne Cahn, "The Role of Congress and the Public in Arms Control," p. 12.

13. *Congress: The Electoral Connection* (New Haven: Yale University Press, 1974).

14. Thomas Dine, "The Issue of Arms Control in the Senate Foreign Relations Committee: Personalities, Politics, and Policy," p. 6.

15. This Senate Foreign Relations Committee disinclination was paralleled by a similar pattern of behavior on the part of the House International Relations Committee (prior to 1975, known as the House Foreign Affairs Committee). The House committee, following the disinterested lead of its chairman, Thomas "Doc" Morgan, by and large was not an active participant in the SALT process during the 1969-76 years.

16. Quoted in Daniel Yergin, "Fulbright's Last Frustration," *The New York Times Magazine*, November 24, 1974, p. 77.

17. *Congressional Record*, January 14, 1969, p. S564.

18. See Chapter 2, pp. 14-15.

19. "Minority Views to Senate Report on the National Commitments Resolution," *Senate Report* 91-129, June 23, 1969.

20. In the case of selective counterforce targeting, there were several high-ranking officials within the Department of Defense who tried to persuade Secretary Schlesinger not to ask Congress for additional monies to implement the new targeting policy. These people argued that the new targeting policy could be carried out in its most important respects without new monies and that requesting appropriations for establishing the new policy would inevitably lead to undesirable congressional involvement in the policy process. In the end, these arguments proved unpersuasive to Schlesinger, who challenged Congress to a national debate on U.S. strategic policy when requesting monies for selective counterforce targeting. Confidential Interview.

6. Epilogue, 1977

U.S.-Soviet efforts to reach a SALT II accord continued throughout 1977, with meetings taking place almost continuously during the May-December period. In all, there were 219 SALT meetings in Geneva in 1977. However, at year's end, no agreement had been concluded and two of the major issues preventing the implementation of the 1974 Vladivostok Accord during the 1975-76 years--the U.S. cruise missile program and the Soviet Backfire bomber--remained among the major issues separating the two sides.

Nineteen seventy-seven was, however, a year quite different from any during the 1969-76 period in terms of Senate participation in the SALT policy-making process. In part, increased Senate involvement in SALT in 1977 was a legacy of the Vietnam and Watergate experiences, which taken together significantly eroded the authority of the executive branch and legitimized an independent, increasingly assertive role for Congress in this country's foreign relations. Put another way, in 1977, there was a pervasive feeling among many members of the Senate and House as well as among the American people that the president no longer was necessarily the best or only source of wisdom on national security matters. The old attitude of legislative helplessness, inattention, and ultimately rubber-stamping the president's foreign policy initiatives was supplanted to a significant extent by a feeling among most senators that the legislative branch ought to have a central voice in the national security decisions of the government. Lamenting what he perceived as Congress' "over-involvement" in the foreign policy area, veteran columnist Joseph Kraft wrote in late 1977 that:

> The true problem is history.... The systematic deceptions of the Johnson and Nixon Administrations--the revelations about wiretaps, assassinations and all that dirty business--forces the Congress to assert itself. It did so, particularly on Vietnam, with success. In consequence, the national security mystique whereby a President was generally given the benefit of the doubt has been shattered. Now foreign policy issues, like pork barrel issues, have

become a fit subject for legislative wheeling and dealing.[1]

Kraft's analysis only tells part of the story. Increased Senate participation in the strategic arms limitation policy process is traceable only in part to the Vietnam and Watergate experiences. It is also due to changed attitudes in the legislative and executive branches with respect to strategic arms policy. In the Senate (and to a significant extent in the House), 1977 witnessed a perceptibly heightened awareness on the part of many members about both the importance of strategic arms issues to this country's foreign relations and their legitimate role in helping set U.S. policy on those issues. Among a number of senators--Frank Church, Dick Clark, John Culver, Gary Hart, Edward Kennedy, Charles Mathias, et al--SALT was viewed as a set of negotiations integrally related to the nation's security and international well-being--in political, military, and economic terms. Senator Clark, for example, summarized the views of a number of senators in a speech in December 1977 when he declared that "failure to achieve a new SALT agreement" soon could have "serious consequences" for the United States and other nations of the world. Clark warned that failure to conclude and ratify an "acceptable" SALT II accord could "engender a strategic arms race more furious than we have seen to date, producing more provocative and destabilizing weapons; increase defense spending in our own and other countries; cast an added pall over the already difficult problem of Soviet-American relations, perhaps, eventuating a return to the confrontations of the high Cold War period; [and] increase the mathematical probability of nuclear war."[2]

To a number of other senators--Jake Garn, Orrin Hatch, S. I. Hayakawa, Henry Jackson, Daniel Patrick Moynihan, John Tower, et al--American SALT policy in 1977 was cause for increasing concern given the administration's seeming conciliatory and over-eager negotiating posture in Geneva and its continued interest in ardently pursuing a détente relationship with the Soviets. These and other like-minded senators led a vigorous effort in early 1977 to deny the positions of chief SALT negotiator and Director of the Arms Control and Disarmament Agency to Paul Warnke, whom they perceived as "soft" toward the Soviet Union.[3] Senator Tower expressed the thoughts of a number of senators when, in a speech on the Senate floor in September, he criticized the Carter administration's stewardship of SALT matters in particular and defense policy in general. Tower remarked:

>...the course of strategic policy under the Carter Administration...is, frankly, an erratic course, substantially altered by decisions which reflect confusion and uncertainty as to the future of our strategic deterrents [sic].... The Soviets are witness to unilateral U.S. concessions

that will have a decided effect upon our side of the strategic equation.... Above all else, I think our Government and particularly our negotiators, must be alert to the necessity--should it arise--to demonstrate to the Soviets our capacity for patience.[4]

Whether supportive or critical of the executive branch's SALT efforts, senators individually and collectively--through the Armed Services, Foreign Relations, and newly-created Intelligence Committees or their subcommittees--participated in 1977 in the SALT policy process to a far greater extent and in far more meaningful ways than they had during any of the previous eight years. Through committee hearings and individual briefings, a large number of senators tried and, to a significant extent, succeeded in keeping themselves informed about the specifics of U.S. SALT policy. In the hearings, particularly, they challenged administration witnesses to explain in detail the executive branch's proposed policies, and in closed-door sessions with officials and in private letters to the president or secretary of state, they questioned and debated the executive branch's goals and the bases underlying these goals. Through public announcements and speeches and through the declassification and public release of hearings with key administration witnesses,[5] they helped to build popular understanding of the policy issues involved. In addition, aided by increasingly expert and specialized staffs[6] and an unprecedented series of leaks of highly sensitive information,[7] they developed and considered alternatives to those policies proposed by the executive and participated in setting the general direction of policy. Through these and other efforts, such as carefully scrutinizing the administration's annual submission of arms control impact statements on major weapons systems, they generally held the executive branch accountable for its stewardship of strategic arms policy. In short, in 1977, the Senate was meaningfully involved in the SALT policy-making process.

These efforts, inspired and carried out by individual senators as well as by the responsible Senate committees or subcommittees, only partially explain increased Senate involvement in the SALT policy-making process in 1977. One must also cite the changed executive branch attitude toward legislative involvement in SALT. Frequently condemning the closed, secretive foreign policy-making process that characterized the Nixon-Ford-Kissinger era, presidential candidate Carter pledged that, if elected, he would bring a new openness to the policy process. Soon after being elected, President Carter, following up on his campaign pledge, met with the Senate Foreign Relations Committee and declared that "my inclination is whenever possible to share the knowledge that I have with you and to seek your advice and counsel." He added, "I will go a second mile to meet with you on this."[8] In mid-1977, President Carter explicitly addressed the matter of congressional and public involvement in SALT in an interview with several television correspondents. He said:

> In the SALT talks, we've developed a comprehensive proposal to present to the Soviets. We are doing it both privately and, to some degree, publicly.... I think it's good to let the American people know the facts behind the controversies and debates. Obviously, when these kinds of debates are made public, it creates an image of confusion and a lack of a comprehensive policy.... We have to put forward ideas and maybe over a period of time we'll have some progress. I think we will. But I've never had any doubt that the American people ought to be as thoroughly informed as possible and also involved in the decision-making process.[9]

An early, concrete indication of the Carter administration's intention to involve Congress closely in the SALT process came just prior to and just after Secretary of State Cyrus Vance's March 1977 trip to the Soviet Union. Theretofore, when Secretary of State Kissinger had gone to Moscow to discuss strategic arms issues, there was generally no prior consultation with Congress about the trip or public discussions of U.S. SALT plans and negotiating positions.

Now, the situation was different. On March 23, Secretary Vance met in closed session for two hours with the Senate Foreign Relations Committee to discuss his forthcoming trip to the Soviet Union. In this session, Vance discussed in detail the U.S. proposals to be made in Moscow. In addition, on the eve of the secretary of state's departure for Moscow, the president took the unusual step of holding a press conference in order to enunciate, among other things, American goals at the forthcoming U.S.-Soviet talks. Taking into account personal letters from Senator Henry Jackson and Congressman Thomas Downey which had been received prior to Vance's departure for Moscow,[10] the president declared that the United States would propose "actual substantial reductions" in the upcoming negotiations. President Carter even saw fit to mention publicly that the United States had a "fall-back" position from the preferred, more sweeping approach which was to be explored initially. The "fall-back" position was, in essence, "to ratify Vladivostok and wait until later to solve some of the most difficult and contentious issues."[11]

Following several days of hard but unsuccessful closed-door negotiating sessions in Moscow, Secretary Vance held a press conference in Moscow. In this March 30 press conference, Secretary Vance went far beyond what the president had publicly stated the week before. Indeed, the secretary laid out in unprecedented detail the U.S. SALT proposals presented in Moscow. He noted that the preferred American option, known as "the comprehensive proposal," contained four elements: 1) substantial reductions in the overall aggregate of strategic delivery vehicles; 2) reductions in the number of large ballistic missile launchers (MLBMs); 3) reductions in the MIRV launcher aggregate; and 4) limitations on the launchers of ICBMs equipped with MIRVs. Vance noted that as an alternative the U.S. put forward "the deferred proposal." Under this plan, the U.S. suggested that consideration of the cruise missile and Backfire bomber issues be deferred and that all of the remaining issues under the 1974 Vladivostok Accord be resolved and a treaty signed. As Secretary Vance summarily declared: "In essence our proposal was: 'Let's sign up what has been agreed at Vladivostok and put aside the cruise missile and get on with SALT III'."[12]

Two days later in Washington, Assistant to the President for National Security Affairs Zbigniew Brzezinski provided the Congress and the press with the detailed numbers involved in the U.S. proposals. Specifically, Brzezinski noted that the United States had proposed in Moscow that the aggregate levels of Vladivostok be reduced from 2,400 to a range between 1,800-2,000 and that the Vladivostok MIRV level of 1,320 be reduced to between 1,100-1,200. Brzezinski also discussed other proposed reductions, including a possible freeze on the development and new technology.[13]

The Soviets rejected both American proposals--the comprehensive and the deferral--but agreed to further talks in Geneva later in the spring. Prior to those talks which took place toward the end of May, Secretary Vance, ACDA Director Warnke, and other officials consulted with various individual senators and interested congressional committees (e.g., Senate Foreign Relations, Senate Armed Services, House International Relations, House Armed Services) to discuss both the American and Soviet negotiating postures at SALT. In the end, the Geneva talks between Secretary Vance and Soviet Foreign Minister Gromyko established a three-tiered framework for all ensuing SALT II negotiations. The first tier consisted of a treaty affirming what had been accomplished at Vladivostok, with a provision calling for roughly ten per cent additional reductions. The second tier was a protocol to take care of many of the difficult, unresolved issues (e.g., cruise missile limitations, mobile missiles, et al.) for a three-year period. The third tier involved guidelines for SALT III--the next round of negotiations--which would cover the remaining issues not dealt with elsewhere in the agreement.[14]

Following the May talks, the two negotiating teams in Geneva settled down to several months of hard, intense bargaining. In early September, when it became clear that the five-year SALT I Interim Agreement would expire on October 3, 1977 and would not be immediately replaced by a new SALT accord, a planned Vance-Gromyko meeting in Vienna was deferred until late September, and Congress was consulted about what to do concerning the pending expiration of the Interim Agreement. It was the executive branch's intention to let the Interim Agreement expire and to issue a unilateral policy declaration which made it clear that the U.S. would "not take any action inconsistent with the provisions of the Interim Agreement and with the goals of these ongoing [SALT] negotiations."[15] It was hoped and expected that the Soviets would do likewise.

It was also the executive's view that since no new, binding agreement had been concluded between the two sides, there was no need for additional congressional action regarding the Interim Agreement. However, in a meeting with the Foreign Relations Committee on September 26, ACDA Director Warnke indicated that if the Senate saw fit to pass a resolution in support of the United States' unilateral declaration of intent, the executive would welcome such legislative action.

In the end, after some debate within the Foreign Relations Committee and on the floor, the Senate enacted without opposition Senate Concurrent Resolution 56. This provided that "the President is authorized to proceed in accordance with the declaration of intent of the Secretary of State of September 21, 1977," and that "the Secretary of State shall at least once every six months during negotiations for a SALT II Agreement report to the Congress on the exact status of negotiations for such a SALT Agreement."[16]

Although Vance and Gromyko did not meet in early September in Vienna as originally planned, they did meet in both Washington and New York during the last week of September. When he was in Washington, Gromyko also had two meetings with President Carter to discuss SALT. Although no SALT II agreement was concluded during the Soviet Foreign Minister's trip, it was widely reported in the press that a good deal of progress had been achieved.[17]

Just following Foreign Minister Gromyko's trip to Washington, an intensive series of briefings of senators and their staffs was initiated to keep Members of Congress informed about the status of the talks and to receive advice regarding future U.S. SALT initiatives. During this early fall period, consultation with the Senate on SALT included:

- Secretaries Vance and Brown testifying before the Senate Armed Services Subcommittee on Arms Control;
- Secretary Vance testifying before the Senate Foreign Relations Committee;
- ACDA Director Warnke testifying before the Senate Foreign Relations Committee;
- ACDA Director Warnke briefing approximately a dozen senators who are not members of the Foreign Relations or Armed Services Committees;
- ACDA Director Warnke briefing roughly thirty Senate staff members in two separate meetings in his office;
- Leslie Gelb, Director of the State Department's Bureau of Politico-Military Affairs, and John Newhouse, Assist-

ant Director of ACDA's Bureau of International Security Programs, briefing a number of senators collectively (all 100 senators had been invited to the briefing);
- Newhouse, Marshall Shulman, Special Assistant to the Secretary of State for Soviet Affairs, and Walter Slocombe, Principal Deputy Assistant Secretary of Defense for International Security Affairs, briefing roughly forty Senate staff members.

At an October 14 hearing before the Armed Services Subcommittee on Arms Control, Secretary Vance offered to consult closely with the subcommittee on SALT in coming weeks and months and subsequently explained his offer and the rationale for the other on-going briefings: "I have offered to meet with them as often as they wish and suggest that we regularize it on a basis that would mean that we would meet at least once every two weeks. I think it is absolutely essential that we do have a complete and full dialogue so that they can understand where we are going and we can have their input into our thinking."[18]

Besides testifying on a regular basis before interested congressional committees and briefing senators and their staffs regularly, the Carter administration undertook in 1977 an unprecedented initiative in an effort to involve Members of Congress closely in the SALT process--a program of official congressional SALT advisers was begun. Several senators had long sought an official advisory role on SALT policy matters. But this goal had been frustrated during the Nixon and Ford administrations, principally due to the objections of Henry Kissinger.[19] In May 1977, the new administration set out to change this. At that time, ACDA Director Warnke wrote to the President of the Senate and the Speaker of the House asking that several members of each house be designated as advisers to the SALT delegation. In his letter, Warnke declared that "although the actual negotiating would have to be done by the Delegation itself, the Congressional advisers could attend as observers the plenary sessions of the Delegations and also attend intra-U.S. Delegation meetings where their comments and advice would be solicited."[20] Also, in Geneva, congressional SALT advisers could read and discuss with delegation members the joint draft text of the emerging SALT II agreement.

The response from the Congress was overwhelmingly favorable. In all, twenty-five senators and fourteen congressmen were designated as official SALT advisers for 1977.[21] Of these, more than one-third actually visited Geneva and participated in the SALT talks. From the executive branch's point of view, the program was viewed as a success as well. Indeed, in late December, Secretary Vance wrote to each member of the Senate who had not yet attended the SALT talks and encouraged them to "come to Geneva to discuss the negotiations with our representatives and those of the Soviet Union."[22]

Whether because of the Vietnam and Watergate experiences,

or because of increasing interest on the part of many senators in U.S. SALT policy, or because of a new administration's changed attitude toward the desirability of active congressional involvement in the policy process, executive-legislative relations regarding SALT in 1977 were characterized by an unprecedented sharing of information between the two branches that helped lead to an unusually high degree of Senate participation in the strategic arms policy-making process. In 1978 and for the foreseeable future, this situation seems likely to continue. Whether this will mean that an eventual SALT II Treaty will be approved by the Senate is uncertain. It is clear, though, that the legislative branch's role in the making of U.S. SALT policy will be far greater than it ever was during the 1969-76 years.

NOTES

1. "It's Time to End 'Congressional Foreign Policy'," WP, October 25, 1977.
2. Remarks of Senator Dick Clark at the Annual Meeting of the Arms Control Association, December 16, 1977.
3. See "Consideration of Mr. Paul C. Warnke to be Director of the U.S. Arms Control and Disarmament Agency and Ambassador," Hearings before the Committee on Armed Services, February 22, 23, 28, 1977, U.S. Senate, 95th Congress, 1st Session (Washington: Government Printing Office, 1977).
4. "Salt Talks," Congressional Record, September 27, 1977, p. S15728.
5. See, for example, "Briefings by Cyrus Vance, Secretary of State, and Ambassador Paul C. Warnke, Director, Arms Control and Disarmament Agency, on the SALT Negotiations, November 3 and November 29, 1977," before the Committee on Foreign Relations, U.S. Senate, 95th Congress, 1st Session (Washington: Government Printing Office, 1978).
6. In 1975, Senate Resolution 60 was enacted which enabled each member of the Foreign Relations Committee (and other major committees) to hire a professional staff member to work full-time for the individual senator on the given committee's work. For a recent discussion of the role of congressional staff in the policy process, see Michael Malbin, "Congressional Committee Staffs: Who's in Charge There?" Public Interest 47 (Spring 1977). For a discussion of the role of congressional staff members in the area of weapons procurement, see John Allsbrook, "Role of Congressional Staff in Weapons System Acquisition," Defense Management Review 1 (Spring 1977), esp. pp. 37-41.
7. See Robert Kaiser, "SALT Talks: Leaking toward Armageddon?" More (February 1978).
8. Quoted in Loch Johnson and James E. McCormick, "Foreign Policy by Executive Fiat," Foreign Policy 28 (Fall 1977), p. 138.

9. "President Carter Interviewed by ABC News Correspondents, August 10, 1977," reprinted in The Department of State Bulletin, September 26, 1977, p. 395.

10. For a discussion of these letters from Senator Jackson and Congressman Downey and their influence on U.S. SALT policy, see Defense and Foreign Affairs Daily 6, no. 224 (November 1977): 1-2.

11. "The President's News Conference of March 24, 1977," Presidential Documents: Jimmy Carter, Vol. 13, No. 15, p. 440.

12. Transcript of the Press Conference of Cyrus Vance, March 30, 1977.

13. Transcript of the Press Conference of Zbigniew Brzezinski, April 1, 1977. For further discussion of the March SALT proposals, see Secretary of Defense Harold Brown's "Defense Planning and Arms Control, Remarks Delivered at the University of Rochester, April 13, 1977." For an in-depth critical appraisal of these proposals, see Paul Nitze's "An Analysis of the Two U.S./Moscow SALT Proposals of March 1977," in Paul Nitze, John F. Lehman, Seymour Weiss, The Carter Disarmament Proposals: Some Basic Questions and Cautions (Center for Advanced International Studies, University of Miami, 1977), pp. 9-17.

14. For further details of this three-tiered framework for SALT II, see "News Conference of Secretary of State Cyrus Vance, May 21, 1977," reprinted in The Department of State Bulletin, June 13, 1977, pp. 628-33.

15. Letter from Secretary of State Cyrus Vance to Senate Foreign Relations Committee Chairman John Sparkman, September 21, 1977.

16. Congressional Record, October 19, 1977, pp. 17372-73.

17. See, for example, NYT, October 11, 1977 and WP, October 12, 1977.

18. Transcript of Secretary Cyrus Vance's Appearance on "Meet the Press," October 16, 1977.

19. See Chapter 2, p. 20.

20. Letter from Paul Warnke to Walter Mondale, President of the Senate, May 9, 1977.

21. The following Senators and Representatives were SALT advisers during 1977: Senators Robert Byrd, Alan Cranston, James Eastland, Hubert Humphrey, Henry Jackson, John Culver, Sam Nunn, Gary Hart, Frank Church, Claiborne Pell, John Glenn, Daniel Inouye, George McGovern, Adlai Stevenson, Howard Baker, Ted Stevens, Milton Young, Clifford Hansen, Clifford Case, Jacob Javits, Barry Goldwater, John Tower, John Chafee, James Pearson, Charles Percy, Charles Mathias, Malcolm Wallop; Representatives Melvin Price, Clement Zablocki, Charles E. Wilson, Jonathan Bingham, Lee Hamilton, Bob Carr, Thomas Downey, Anthony Beilenson, William Broomfield, John Anderson, John Buchanan, Manual Lujan, Elwood Hillis, and Richard Schultze.

22. Circular letter from Secretary of State Cyrus Vance encouraging senators to attend SALT, December 28, 1977.

Selected Bibliography

BOOKS

Aldridge, Robert. The Counterforce Syndrome. Washington: Transnational Institute, 1978.

Ball, Desmond. Déja Vu: The Return to Counterforce in the Nixon Administration. Los Angeles: Southern California Seminar on Arms Control, 1974.

Barton, John, and Weiler, Lawrence, eds. International Arms Control: Issues and Agreements. Stanford: Stanford University Press, 1976.

Bliss, Howard, and Johnson, Glen. Beyond the Water's Edge: America's Foreign Policies. Philadelphia: Lippincott and Company, 1975.

Brandon, Henry. The Retreat of American Power. New York: Dell Publishing Co., 1972.

Cahn, Anne. Congress, the Military and Information. Beverly Hills, California: Sage Publications, #04-017, 1974.

Chayes, Abram, and Wiesner, Jerome, eds. ABM: An Evaluation of the Decision to Deploy an Anti-Ballistic Missile System. New York: Harper, 1969.

Clotfelter, James. The Military in American Politics. Chapel Hill: University of North Carolina Press, 1973.

Davis, Lynn. Limited Nuclear Options, Adelphi Paper #121. London: International Institute for Strategic Studies, 1976.

Dodd, Lawrence, and Oppenheimer, Bruce, eds. Congress Reconsidered. New York: Praeger, 1977.

Fisher, Louis. President and Congress. New York: Free Press, 1972.

Frye, Alton. A Responsible Congress: The Politics of National Security. New York: McGraw-Hill, 1976.

Gompert, David, et al. Nuclear Weapons and Foreign Policy. New York: McGraw-Hill, 1977.

Greenwood, Ted. Making the MIRV: A Study in Defense Decision Making. Cambridge, Massachusetts: Ballinger Publishing Co., 1975.

Halperin, Morton. Bureaucratic Politics and Foreign Policy Washington: The Brookings Institution, 1974.

Hammond, Paul. *Cold War and Détente*. New York: Harcourt, Brace and Jovanovich, 1975.

Henkin, Louis. *Foreign Affairs and the Constitution*. New York: Norton, 1972.

Huntington, Samuel. *The Common Defense*. New York: Columbia University Press, 1961.

Jackson, Henry, ed. *The National Security Council*. New York: Praeger, 1965.

Kahan, Jerome. *Security in the Nuclear Age*. Washington: The Brookings Institution, 1975.

Kalb, Marvin, and Kalb, Bernard. *Kissinger*. Boston: Little, Brown and Co., 1974.

Kaplan, Morton A., ed. *SALT: Problems and Prospects*. Morristown, New Jersey: General Learning Press, 1973.

Kintner, William R., and Pfaltzgraff, Robert, Jr., eds. *SALT: Implications for Arms Control in the 1970s*. Pittsburgh: University of Pittsburgh Press, 1973.

Kissinger, Henry. *American Foreign Policy*. New York: Norton, 1974.

Lehman, John. *The Executive, Congress and Foreign Policy*. New York: Praeger, 1976.

Long, Franklin, and Rathjens, George, eds. *Arms, Defense Policy, and Arms Control*. New York: Norton, 1975.

Mayhew, David. *Congress: The Electoral Connection*. New Haven: Yale University Press, 1974.

Morris, Roger. *Uncertain Greatness: Henry Kissinger and American Foreign Policy*. New York: Harper and Row, 1977.

Muskie, Edmund, and Brock, Bill. *What Price Defense?* Washington: American Enterprise Institute, 1974.

Nathan, James, and Oliver, James. *United States Foreign Policy and World Order*. Boston: Little, Brown and Co., 1976.

Newhouse, John. *Cold Dawn: The Story of SALT*. New York: Holt, Rinehart and Winston, 1975.

Nitze, Paul, Lehman, John, and Weiss, Seymour. *The Carter Disarmament Proposals: Some Basic Questions and Cautions*. Miami: Center for Advanced International Studies of the University of Miami, 1977.

Ognibene, Peter. *Scoop: The Life and Times of Henry M. Jackson*. New York: Stein and Day, 1975.

Ogul, Morris. *Congress Oversees the Bureaucracy*. Pittsburgh: University of Pittsburgh Press, 1976.

Orenstein, Norman, ed. *Congress in Change*. New York: Praeger, 1975.

Orfield, Gary. *Congressional Power: Congress and Social Change*. New York: Harcourt, Brace and Jovanovich, 1975.

Pfaltzgraff, Robert, Jr., ed. *Contrasting Approaches to Strategic Arms Control*. Lexington, Massachusetts: Lexington Books, 1974.

_____ and Davis, Jacquelyn. *SALT II: Promise or Precipice?* Miami: University of Miami Press, 1976.

Platt, Alan, and Weiler, Lawrence, eds., *Congress and Arms*

Control. Boulder, Colorado: Westview Press, 1978.
Pranger, Robert, and Labrie, Roger, eds. Nuclear Strategy and National Security: Points of View. Washington: American Enterprise Institute, 1977.
Report of the Commission on the Organization of the Government for the Conduct of Foreign Policy. 7 volumes. Washington: Government Printing Office, 1975.
Roberts, Charles, ed. Has the President Too Much Power? New York: Harper and Row, 1974.
Schlesinger, Arthur, Jr. The Imperial Presidency. Boston: Houghton, Mifflin and Co., 1973.
Slocombe, Walter. The Political Implications of Strategic Parity, Adelphia Paper #77. London: International Institute for Strategic Studies, 1971.
Smith, Gerard. SALT: The First Strategic Arms Negotiations. New York: Doubleday and Co., forthcoming.
Stennis, John, and Fulbright, J. William. The Role of Congress in Foreign Policy. Washington: American Enterprise Institute, 1971.
Strategic Arms Limitation Talks (SALT): Legislative History of the Jackson Amendment, 1972.
Weiler, Lawrence. The Arms Race, Secret Negotiations, and the Congress, Occasional Paper #12. The Stanley Foundation, 1977.
Wilcox, Francis. Congress, the Executive and Foreign Policy. New York: Harper and Row, 1971.
_____ and Frank, Richard, eds. The Constitution and the Conduct of Foreign Policy. New York: Praeger, 1976.
Willrich, Mason, and Rhinelander, John, eds. SALT: The Moscow Agreements and Beyond. New York: Free Press, 1974.
Wolfe, Thomas. The SALT Experience: Its Impact on U.S. and Soviet Strategic Policy and Decision-Making. Santa Monica, California: The Rand Corporation, R 1686-PR, 1975.

ARTICLES

Allsbrook, John. "Role of Congressional Staffs in Weapon System Acquisition." Defense Systems Management Review 1 (Spring 1977).
Aspin, Les. "SALT II or No SALT,' Report issued by the Office of Congressman Les Aspin, January 1978.
_____. "The Defense Budget and Foreign Policy: The Role of Congress." Daedalus (Summer 1975).
_____. "Why Doesn't Congress Do Something?" Foreign Policy, no. 15 (Summer 1974).
Bax, Frans. "The Legislative-Executive Relationship in Foreign Policy: New Partnership or New Competition?" Orbis 20 (Winter 1977).
Bell, Robert, "Implications of Extending the SALT I Interim Agreement." Published by the Congressional Research Serv-

ice, Library of Congress, May 1977.

Benson, Robert. "The Military on Capitol Hill: Prospectors in Quest for Funds." Annals of the American Academy of Political and Social Science (March 1973).

Burt, Richard. "The Risks of Asking SALT to Do Too Much." The Washington Review 1 (January 1978).

Cahn, Anne. "The Role of Congress and the Public in Arms Control." Unpublished paper, Harvard University, 1974.

Carter, Barry. "Nuclear Strategy and Nuclear Weapons. Scientific American 230 (May 1974).

Carter, Luther, "Beyond Vladivostok: The Feasibility and the Policies of Arms Reductions." Science 187 (April 11, 1975).

Cronin, Richard. "An Analysis of Congressional Reductions in the Defense Budget; Fiscal Years 1971-1976." Published by the Congressional Research Service, Library of Congress, 1976.

Dine, Thomas. "A Primer for Capitol Hill." The New York Times, April 4, 1975.

_____. "Military R&D: Congress' Next Area of Policy Penetration." Bulletin of the Atomic Scientists 34, no. 2 (February 1978).

_____. "The Issue of Arms Control in the Senate Foreign Relations Committee." Unpublished paper, Harvard University, 1975.

Drell, Sidney, and von Hippel, Frank. "Limited Nuclear War." Scientific American 235 (November 1976).

Drew, Elizabeth. "An Argument over Survival." The New Yorker (April 4, 1977).

Flanagan, Stephen. "Congress and the Carter Administration's Policy in SALT: The New Politics of Arms Control." Paper delivered at the Annual Meeting of the International Studies Association, Washington, D.C., February 1978.

Frye, Alton. "Congressional Politics and Policy Analysis: Bridging the Gap." Policy Analysis 2 (Spring 1976).

Garthoff, Raymond. "Negotiating with the Russians: Some Lessons from SALT." International Security 1, no. 4 (Spring 1977).

Gelb, Leslie. "The Story of a Flap." Foreign Policy, no. 16 (Fall 1974).

Gray, Colin. "Detente, Arms Control and Strategy: Perspectives on SALT." American Political Science Review 70, no. 6 (December 1976).

_____. "Who's Afraid of the Cruise Missile?" Orbis 21 (Fall 1977).

Hallett, Douglas. "Kissinger Colossus: The Domestic Politics of SALT." The Yale Review 65 (Winter 1976).

Halsted, Thomas. "Lobbying against the ABM, 1967-70." Bulletin of the Atomic Scientists 27 (April 1971).

Ikle, Fred. "Can Deterrence Last Out the Century? Foreign Affairs 52 (Winter 1973).

_____. "What to Hope for, and Worry About, in SALT." *Fortune* (October 1977).
Johnson, Loch, and McCormick, James. "Foreign Policy by Executive Fiat." *Foreign Policy* 28 (Fall 1977).
Kaiser, Robert. "SALT Talks: Leaking toward Armageddon?" *More* (February 1978).
Kistiakowsky, G.B. "The Arms Race: Is Paranoia Necessary for Security?" *The New York Times Magazine* (November 27, 1977).
Kondracke, Morton. "The Assault on SALT." *The New Republic* (December 12, 1977).
Korb, Lawrence. "The Bicentennial Defense Budget: A Critical Appraisal." *Armed Forces and Society* 2 (November 1975).
Kruzel, Joseph. "SALT II: The Search for a Follow-On Agreement." *Orbis* 17 (Summer 1973).
Laird, Melvin. "Arms Control: The Russians are Cheating?" *The Reader's Digest* (December 1977).
Lauk, Kurt. "Possibilities of Senatorial Influence: The Case of the Jackson Amendment to SALT I." Unpublished paper, Stanford University, 1975.
Laurance, Edward. "The Changing Role of Congress in Defense Policy-Making." *Journal of Conflict Resolution* 20 (June 1976).
Lodal, Jan. "Verifying SALT." *Foreign Policy* 24 (Fall 1976).
Luttwak, Edward. "Why Arms Control Has Failed." *Commentary* 65, no. 1 (January 1978).
Malbin, Michael. "Congressional Committee Staffs: Who's in Charge There?" *Public Interest* 47 (Spring 1977).
Medalia, Jonathan. "The U.S. Senate and Strategic Arms Limitation Policy Making, 1963-1972." Unpublished Ph.D. Dissertation, Stanford University, 1975.
Mitchell, Douglas. "Executive Branch Organization for the Planning and Conduct of SALT." Published by the Congressional Research Service, Library of Congress, September 1977.
Murphy, John. "Knowledge is Power: Foreign Policy and Information Interchange Among Congress, the Executive Branch and the Public." *Tulane Law Review* 49 (March 1975).
Nitze, Paul. "Assuring Strategic Stability in an Era of Détente." *Foreign Affairs* 54 (January 1976).
_____. "Current SALT II Negotiating Posture." Statement issued at press conference, November 1, 1977.
Scoville, Herbert, Jr. "Flexible MADness." *Foreign Policy* 14 (Spring 1974).
Smith, Gerard. "SALT After Vladivostok." *Journal of International Affairs* 29 (Spring 1975).
Sonnenfeldt, Helmut. "Russia, America and Detente." *Foreign Affairs* 56, no. 2 (January 1978).
Stern, Paula. "The Water's Edge: The Jackson Amendment as a Case Study to the Role Domestic Politics Plays in the Creation of American Foreign Policy." Unpublished Ph.D. Dissertation, The Fletcher School of Law and Diplomacy, 1976.

Stone, Jeremy. "Autumn Washington with a Grain of SALT." *Federation of American Scientists' Public Interest Report* 31 (January 1978).

Van Cleave, William, and Barnett, Roger. "Strategic Adaptability." *Orbis* 15 (Fall 1974).

Warnke, Paul. "Apes on a Treadmill." *Foreign Policy* 18 (Spring 1975).

Whitehurst, William, et al. "Can the Arms Race be Ended?" Government Printing Office, 1974.

Yergin, Daniel. "Fulbright's Last Frustration." *The New York Times Magazine* (November 24, 1974).

Index

ABM. See Antiballistic Missile
Agreement on the Prevention of Nuclear War, 44
Aiken, A., U.S. Senator, 77
Albert, C., U.S. Senator, 16
Antiballistic Missile, 12, 14, 15, 17, 19, 22
  debates on, xi, xiii, 1-4
  ratification of, 25
  Protocol to 1972 Treaty, 57
Armed Services Committee, 6, 19, 26, 74, 82
Armed Services Subcommittee on Research and Development, 84, 90, 91, 103, 105
  defense budget hearings, 82
Armed Services Subcommittee on SALT, 20, 21, 59, 74
  testimony of Paul Nitze, 57
Arms Control, defined, 2n3
Arms Control and Disarmament Act, of 1961, 58
Arms Control and Disarmament Agency, U.S., xi, xiii, 9, 16, 22, 42, 98
  Jackson's criticism of, 29
  role of in SALT II, 38-39
Arms Control Associaton, 4
Ash, R., OMB Director, 38
Atlantic Alliance, 26
Behr, R., Asst. Dir. for Weapons Evaluation and Control, ACDA, 40-41
Brezhnev, L., Gen. Secretary, USSR, 21, 25, 42, 44, 57
  and U.S. SALT II proposal, 61

Brooke, E., U.S. Senator, 14, 17, 29, 102
  and counterforce capability, 74-76
Brzezinski, Z., National Security Affairs Advisor, 114
Buckley, J., U.S. Senator,
  proposal to increase counterforce capability, 74
Carter Administration, 6
  and SALT, 111, 112, 113, 114, 115
Case, C., U.S. Senator, 16, 38, 47, 55, 65, 74, 77
  request for briefing on counterforce weapons, 86-87
Center for Defense Information, 4
Colby, William, Director, CIA, 76, 77
Command Data Buffer System, 73
Congress, U.S., role in strategic arms policy, 1-7
  see also Senate, U.S.
Congressional Budget Office, 4
Cooper, J., U.S. Senator, 2, 5, 16, 18
  role in SALT, 19-20, 30
Council for a Livable World, 2, 4
Cranston, A., U.S. Senator, 64, 65, 91, 102
Dobrynin, A., Soviet Ambassador, 17, 57
Essential Equivalence, Schlesinger defines, 52

125

Executive-Legislative Relations, 6
  role of in SALT I, 5, 9-31, 99-107
  role of in SALT II, 5, 37-65, 99-107
  new era of, 46-49
  and national security, 53-54
  role of in counterforce capabilities discussions, 75-80
Executive privilege, 46, 98
Federation of American Scientists, 4
Ford, Gerald, President, 59, 61, 65, 97, 98
  presides over NSC meetings, 60
Foreign Relations Committee, 2, 3, 6, 9, 14, 19, 98, 112
  and Interim Agreement, 25-29
  confirmation of U. Alexis Johnson, 37-38
  and SALT II hearings, 43-44
  and Kissinger, 46-49, 54-56, 58-59
  and lack of leadership on SALT, 101-103
  and Vance discussions, 113-14
Foreign Relations Subcommittee on Arms Control, xiii, 9, 14, 38, 55, 84, 85
  Schlesinger testimony, 52, 77-81, 87-88
  efforts to control SALT policies, 103-107
  Vance hearings, 116
Forward-based systems, 23, 37
Fulbright, W., U.S. Senator, 16, 18, 27, 28, 77, 88, 89
  and Iklé nomination, 41-42
  lack of leadership, 101-103
Geneva, 37, 38, 39, 45, 47, 51, 57, 60, 80, 111
Gore, A., U.S. Senator, 9, 14
Government Operations Subcommittee on National Security and International Operations, 20

Gromyko, A., Foreign Minister, 57, 115
  and U.S. SALT proposal, 61
Helms, R., CIA Director, 11, 12, 19
Helsinki, 9, 19, 20
Humphrey, H., U.S. Senator, 18, 52, 55, 65, 74, 77, 90, 106
  and Iklé nomination, 41-42
ICBM. See Intercontinental ballistic missile
Iklé, F., Director, ACDA, appointment, 30, 40
  confirmation hearings delayed, 41-43
Intercontinental ballistic missile, xi, 15, 19, 23, 37
  limits of in SALT II, 22
  and numerical equality, 26-27
  and Soviet capabilities, 77
Interim Agreement on Offensive Weapons, 22, 23, 24, 51, 58, 59, 65, 76
  and Nixon Administration, 25-29
Jackson, H., U.S. Senator, role in SALT, 19-21, 24, 57, 65, 74, 85, 90, 103, 106
  and amendments to Interim Agreement, 25-29, 44
  proposal for SALT II, 52-53
  criticizes Nixon approach to SALT II, 56-59
  criticizes SALT I, 58
  criticizes Vladivostok Accord, 61-62
Johnson, A., Director, SALT Negotiations, appointed to SALT delegation, 29
  relationship with Senate committees, 37-39, 47, 48, 102
Katz, A., Asst. Dir. for Science and Technology, ACDA, 40-41
Kennedy, E., U.S. Senator, 62, 64, 65, 74, 89, 91, 102, 106
Kissinger, H., Sec. of State, mentioned passim,
  nomination as Secretary of

Kissinger (cont.)
    State, 44-49
    1974 proposal for SALT II, 54-55
    differences with Schlesinger, 55, 60
    and Dobrynin loophole, 57-58
    and Vladivostok Accord, 62-64
    testimony on strategic policy, 82-84
    and control of SALT negotiations, 97-103
Kosygin, A., Premier, USSR, 17
Laird, M., Sec. Defense, 43
    testimony before Senate Armed Services Committee 24
Limited Test Ban Treaty, xi, 2
Lynn, Lawrence, Senior White House Staff on SALT, 11
Mansfield, M., U.S. Senator, 9, 20, 25, 29
Mathias, C., U.S. Senator, 62, 65, 74, 102
McCormack, M., U.S. Senator, 16
McIntyre, J., U.S. Senator, 90, 91, 103, 106
McIntyre-Brooke Amendment, 85
McMahon Act, of 1954, 2
Members of Congress for Peace Through Law, 4
MIRV. See Multiple independently targetable reentry vehicle
Missile,
    air-launched cruise, xi
    intermediate-range ballistic, xi
    medium-range ballistic, xi
    modern large ballistic, xi
    nuclear-powered ballistic submarine, xi
Mitchell, J., U.S. Attorney General, 11
Mondale, W., U.S. Senator, 62, 65, 74, 102
Moorer, T., Admiral, 24

Multiple Independently Targetable Re-entry Vehicle, xi, 11
    negotiations on, 14n16, 15, 17, 18, 19, 23
    and SALT II, 37, 51, 54
    Soviet capability, 47, 50, 77, 79, 81
    arms race, 60
    and Vladivostok Accord, 61-63
Muskie, E., U.S. Senator, xiii, 18, 28, 40, 52, 55, 65, 74, 77, 83, 102
    quest for SALT II briefing, 38-39
    and Iklé nomination, 41-42
    briefing on SALT II, 47-48
    and hearings on counterforce strategies, 78-80
Mutual Balanced Force Reductions, xi
National Command Authority, 12
NATO. See North Atlantic Treaty Organization
Nitze, P., Asst. Sec. of Defense for SALT, 24, 47, 48, 80
Nixon Administration, 9, 10, 22, 56, 97, 99
    efforts to convince Congress to ratify SALT I, 22-29
Nixon, R.M., U.S. President, informs public of SALT I Accord, 21-24
    discussions with Senator Jackson, 27-30
    and Declaration of Basic Principles of Mutual Relations with USSR, 29, 44-45, 49
    and preoccupations, 50
    1973 Foreign Policy Report to Congress, 51
    State of World Message, 72
    and 1972 Summit agreement, 57
    and 1974 Summit agreements, 57
Non-Proliferation Treaty, xi, 2

North Atlantic Treaty Organization, xi, 16
Office of Technology Assessment, xi, 4
 and criticisms of Department of Defense estimates of casualties from nuclear exchange, 88-90
Packard, D., Dep. Sec. of Defense, 11
Peaceful Nuclear Explosion, xi
Pell, C., U.S. Senator, 23, 77, 87
Proxmire, W., U.S. Senator, 53
Richardson, E., Under Sec. of State, 11, 43-44
Rogers, W., Sec. of State, 24
 testimony, 43
SALT I, mentioned passim,
 White House control over, 10-31, 97-107
 U.S. options for, 12-13
 secret pledges made, 57-59
 see also, Executive-Legislative relations, and Senate, U.S.
SALT II, mentioned passim,
 initial negotiations, 37
 Soviet delegation to, 37
 use of bargaining chip, 39-40
 White House briefings on, 44-45
 1973 session, 50
 1974 session resumed, 60
 relationship to counterforce capabilities, 80-81
 efforts to reach accord, 110-11
 see also, Executive-Legislative relations, and Senate, U.S.
SALT III, 114
SALT Policy Making Process,
 efforts of Executive and Senate to control, 97-107

SALT Policy Making (cont.)
 assertive role of Congress, 110-117
SALT Verification Panel Working Group, 10-12, 15, 98
Schlesinger, J., Defense Sec., 5, 44, 50, 54, 74, 76, 102
 differences with Kissinger, 51, 55, 60
 defines "essential equivalence," 52
 announces counterforce options, 71-73, 75
 hearings on counterforce options, 77-81
 briefing on counterforce options, 86-88
Scott, H., U.S. Senator, 27, 29
Seamons, R., 14
Selective Counterforce Targeting, 5
 change in policy, 71-74
 Schlesinger testimony, 78-80
 relationship to SALT II, 80-81
 Senate efforts to make policy on, 104-107
 see also, Senate, U.S.
Senate, U.S., role in American foreign policy, mentioned passim,
 role in SALT I, 4, 5, 19-31
 role in SALT II, 4, 5, 6, 41-65
 role in selective counterforce targeting, 5, 74-92
 see also, Executive-Legislative relations, and SALT I, II
Senate Resolution 20, 63-65
Senate Resolution 211, 14-15
Senate Resolution 283, 53
Senate Resolution 399, 64
Sense of the Senate Legislation, 14, 52, 62, 102, 103, 107
Single Integrated Operational Plan (SIOP), 72-73
SLBM. See Submarine-launched

SLBM (cont.)
  ballistic missile
Smith, G., Director, ACDA, 9, 11, 13, 16, 17, 19, 20, 24, 29, 98
  leaves office, 37
Soviet Union, 10, 11, 15, 24, 25, 26, 46
  negotiations with U.S., 5, 13, 45, 50, 110
  first strike potential, 75
  build up of counterforce programs, 90
Stanford University Arms Control and Disarmament Program, xiii, xiv
Stennis, J., U.S. Senator, 16, 24, 85
Strategic Air Command, 73
Submarine-launched ballistic missile, xi, 19
  limit of in SALT I, 22
  and numerical equality, 26-27
Symington, Stuart, U.S. Senator, 28, 39, 77, 87, 90, 102
  confirmation hearings of Kissinger, 46
  criticizes SALT I, 58
Threshold Test Ban Treaty, xi
Tower, J., U.S. Senator, 24, 85, 103, 111
Treaty on the Limitation of Underground Nuclear Weapons, 57
Vance, C., Sec. of State, 113, 115
Vienna, 9, 12, 13, 14, 15, 16, 17, 19, 20
Vladivostok Accord, 61-65, 90, 110, 114
War Powers Act, xiii
Warnke, P., Chief SALT negotiator, 111, 116
Weiler, L., SALT delegation member, 32n16, 98
Wheeler, E., Chairman, Joint Chiefs of Staff, 11, 12

JX
1974.75
P56

JX   Platt, Alan
1974.75
P56   The U.S. Senate and
            strategic arms
            policy, 1969-1977